"Ladies and Gentlemen, strap in for a no-nonsense, gut-punching dive into the heart of American liberty with Josh Bernstein's *Preserving Liberty*! Bernstein, a fierce patriot with a knack for cutting through the BS, delivers a blistering critique of the creeping socialism threatening to dismantle our beloved freedoms. His unapologetic, in-your-face style will resonate with every American who's fed up with the establishment's lies and power grabs. This book is your battle cry in the fight to save our nation's soul—prepare to be awakened, enraged, and inspired to reclaim the liberty our Founding Fathers fought so hard to secure."

—Roger Stone, *New York Times* bestselling author

"Josh Bernstein puts real investigation into investigative journalism."

—Alan Dershowitz, attorney and *New York Times* bestselling author

"Josh Bernstein and I have been fighting to expose the Covid cover-up, and I am happy to fight alongside him."

—Dr. Pierre Kory, world-renowned critical care specialist and author of *The War on Ivermectin*

"Like me, Josh understands how it is to be falsely accused and then proven innocent. Josh Bernstein's exoneration from false attacks is *Preserving Liberty*."

—Fred Galvin, major USMC (retired) and author of *A Few Bad Men*

"Like myself, Josh Bernstein covers the important issues of our times with cold, hard facts. His work uncovers many uncomfortable truths."

—Edward Dowd, founder of Phinance Technologies and author of *Cause Unknown*

"At last! Some solutions! We all know America is in trouble, but what to do? Josh Bernstein has opened up the debate. Lots of great ideas presented with clarity and vision. Thank you, Josh!"

—Trevor Loudon, filmmaker, author, and speaker

"Josh Bernstein was dominating the alternative media landscape while many people were still trusting the mainstream narrative with pacifiers in their mouths. His new book, *Preserving Liberty*, continues that tradition as a hard-hitting truth teller that you cannot miss!"

—A. J. Rice, president and CEO of Publius PR and author of *The White Privilege Album*

"As a sheriff, I need to be tough. Josh Bernstein is one tough investigative journalist with the grit and determination of a sheriff."

—Mark Lamb, state senate candidate and sheriff

"Josh is a constituent in my rural district who I've known for years. He loves his country and seeks the truth always."

—**Wendy Rogers, state senator and Lt. Col. USAF (retired)**

"I have known Josh for many years, and he is one of the few journalists I trust."

—**Sonny Borrelli, state senate majority leader**

"I've known Josh for many years, and no one fights harder to uncover corruption and lies quite like him."

—**Anthony Kern, congressional candidate and state senator**

"Like me, Josh Bernstein has one agenda, to the truth."

— **Ben Bergquam, founder of Frontline America and host of *Law and Border***

"Investigative journalist Josh Bernstein has written a few articles for my website. Each one on topics important to defending our liberties."

—**Jim Hoft, cofounder and editor of TGP**

"Josh Bernstein has been an all-star guest on my program since 2015. My audience and I love his no-holds-barred approach to tackling the issues of our time with intellect and facts."

—**Jeff Crouere, radio talk show host and station owner of WGSO 990 in Louisiana**

"Josh Bernstein and I go way back. 2014, I think. One thing I can say about him is that he is like a pit bull, relentless salivating to get at the truth."

—**James Lowe, host of the *Jiggy Jaguar Show***

"Josh Bernstein is a dynamic American newsman, whom I just got to know recently. We in Australia love his commentary, and he is my go-to source for breaking news in the United States."

—**Jason Olbourne, TNT radio presenter**

"I'm known for climbing some of the highest buildings and skyscrapers to save the lives of unborn children. Josh Bernstein climbs onto the backs of corrupt politicians and holds them all accountable."

—**Maison Deschamps, pro-life Spiderman**

PRESERVING LIBERTY

LIBERTY

BOLD AND BRAVE SOLUTIONS TO SAVE AMERICA AND CREATE PERMANENT FREEDOM

JOSH BERNSTEIN

Skyhorse Publishing

Skyhorse Publishing books may be purchased in bulk at special discounts for sales promotion, corporate gifts, fund-raising, or educational purposes. Special editions can also be created to specifications. For details, contact the Special Sales Department, Skyhorse Publishing, 307 West 36th Street, 11th Floor, New York, NY 10018 or info@skyhorsepublishing.com.

Skyhorse® and Skyhorse Publishing® are registered trademarks of Skyhorse Publishing, Inc.®, a Delaware corporation.

Visit our website at www.skyhorsepublishing.com.

Please follow our publisher Tony Lyons on Instagram @tonylyonsisuncertain.

10 9 8 7 6 5 4 3 2 1

Library of Congress Cataloging-in-Publication Data is available on file.

Hardcover ISBN: 978-1-5107-8219-8
eBook ISBN: 978-1-5107-8221-1

Cover design by Brian Peterson

Printed in the United States of America

Contents

Foreword by Congressman Paul Gosar   *vii*

Introduction   *ix*

Chapter One: Restoring Voter Confidence and Integrity   1

Chapter Two: Unintended Consequences of Big Government   23

Chapter Three: Closing Our Borders   35

Chapter Four: Dismantling Washington, DC   47

Chapter Five: Houston, We Have a Spending Problem   59

Chapter Six: An Armed Society Is a Polite Society   71

Chapter Seven: Lab Leak or Wet Market? The Origins of Covid-19   85

Chapter Eight: The China Syndrome   109

Chapter Nine: The Class Warfare Argument and Universal Basic Income   127

Chapter Ten: Censorship, Fake News, and How to Fix It All   135

Conclusion: Preserving Liberty   155

Notes   159

Acknowledgments   167

About the Author   175

Foreword

By Congressman Paul Gosar

What does it really mean to preserve liberty?
How do we preserve our liberties and our God-given rights, when those whom we elected to protect them, instead want to take them from us?

We preserve our liberties by ensuring that our freedoms enshrined in our Bill of Rights and Constitution are upheld and not eroded over time.

We preserve our liberties by preventing excessive government overreach and intrusive intervention in our lives.

We preserve our liberties by maintaining and reinforcing an electoral process that is transparent, free from corruption, and fair for all.

We preserve our liberties by encouraging personal responsibility and accountability by teaching that freedom is the result of the first of those two actions.

We preserve our liberties by putting our liberties first.

The marketplace of ideas is saturated with books from political pundits and so-called experts, each claiming to have the answers to our nation's problems, however, most of them typically come up short.

Josh Bernstein's *Preserving Liberty* is one of those rare exceptions.

In his debut work, Bernstein doesn't just scratch the surface like so many others, he actually digs deep and provides a comprehensive and achievable blueprint for overhauling our entire political system.

Bernstein provides close to forty real and achievable liberty-based solutions, including ten legislative proposals that if introduced and became law, would have every member of the Washington, DC establishment buying stock in Alka-Seltzer and updating their resumes.

Preserving Liberty is not just another dust collector to be placed on the shelf; it is a gutsy call to action, so radically different, and exactly what our country needs, and at the right time.

Preserving Liberty takes a sledgehammer to the status quo and officially puts the bureaucracy in Washington on notice.

Introduction

In order to show the potentialities of a brighter future, we must first resuscitate the visions of a better past.

—Josh Bernstein

On September 17, 1787, during the final days of the Constitutional Convention, while the delegates were set on drafting the new Constitution of the United States, an important and historical conversation took place just outside the hall. A wealthy socialite by the name of Elizabeth Willing Powel, highly influential in Philadelphia's social circles at the time, approached Benjamin Franklin as he was leaving the convention.

According to most historical accounts, she asked him one of the most important questions in America's infancy. "Well, Doctor Franklin, what have we got, a republic or a monarchy?" The question was direct, teeming with anxiety, the kind one would expect that comes along with the birth of a new nation.

Franklin replied, "A Republic, if you can keep it." With a sense of intrigue and confusion she replied, "Dr. Franklin, why would we not be able to keep it?" What Franklin said next rings true to the present day. "Because the people, on tasting the dish, are always disposed to eat more of it then does them good."

It is amazing that Franklin had the vision to see the trials and tribulations that this brand-new Republic could face in the future. As a man who understood human nature, his warnings were prophetic.

The Framers of our Constitution were such visionaries. They possessed the passion, drive, and determination to create a government that truly represented the people. They were intelligent, selfless, and patriotic. To think that our Founding Fathers, of which Franklin was one, had the foresight to create a new nation and simultaneously developed safeguards to protect our newfound freedoms.

But here we are, two hundred forty-eight years later, and Franklin's premonitions about the future of this great country seem to hit home harder now more than ever before. We are, at this juncture in time, at the precipice of Franklin's warning, feasting on the dish like a prisoner's last meal.

In fact, if you listen closely, you can still hear Franklin's prediction that if we do not maintain the balance of power that the Framers sought to establish in regard to limits on government, then those whom we elect to serve as servants to the people will instead become our masters.

Our God-given freedoms, liberties, and traditions are all under constant attack. Our self-serving politicians in both parties are a big part of the problem. This is happening due to ill-informed people who have been completely disengaged from the political process. This book aims to get those people engaged and focused once again.

In writing this book, my number one objective was to add to the lexicon a mix of bold ideas and brave solutions for what ails our great country. From the moment I sat down to write, my goal was to impart to the readers a deeper understanding of many of the issues we face. Moreover, I aimed to pinpoint the different obstacles and roadblocks in our way to creating permanent freedom for every American at the expense of our elected leaders.

My hope is to educate, motivate, cultivate, and activate millions of American citizens to act by introducing these ideas and proposals to their members of Congress, their state representatives, or if necessary, to demand action through the development of petitions for ballot measures that can be taken directly to the voters.

A good idea can only become a great idea when it is acted upon. When these ideas go from concepts to reality, they will help bring back fiscal sanity, judicial fairness, law and order, election integrity, and preserve liberty and freedom for every single American.

The two-party duopoly, which has ruled Washington, DC for many decades, as well as the military industrial complex and the entrenched administrative state will likely take issue with these proposals because they are specifically designed to upend and dismantle their grip on power.

As Ronald Reagan once famously said, "In this present crisis, government is not the solution to our problems. Government is the problem." He then continued, "From time to time we've been tempted to believe that society has become too complex to be managed by self-rule and that government by an elite group is superior to government for, by, and of the people."[1]

Chalk up another win for the Gipper, as he was right. In addition to Ronald Reagan's warnings about big government, here is an aphorism of my very own: "Those who have the power to govern themselves govern best."

In this examination and autopsy of today's United States of America, I will attempt to discuss our most pressing issues. Issues so pressing that if America does not change course soon, there might not be much liberty left for us to preserve.

I will help expose those who wish to keep us in the dark and under their control and thoroughly dissect the known cancer that is metastasizing itself into our lives and our government. In addition, I will provide sound, logical, and liberty-based solutions to many of the problems America faces.

Now, let's turn our focus and attention onto the millions of Americans who are sick and tired of being sick and tired. Let's focus our attention on those Americans who feel most forgotten and like strangers in their own states. Those Americans who live out in the country on farms, or in our more sparsely populated areas, far away from the closest big city.

Those Americans who, sadly, no longer have their voices heard in what is supposed to be a representative government. Those Americans whose voices and votes no longer really count due to their physical locations. Those Americans who may vote in every election, but their votes are canceled out by large, populated cities in their states.

This book is dedicated to you.

To those Americans, who feel as though they went to bed and woke up to a different country. To those Americans, who feel as though America's traditions, customs, and values are under constant assault by a ruling political class completely out of touch with most of the people.

To those Americans who firmly believe in limited government, law and order, securing our borders, free speech, the Second Amendment and upholding our values and our Constitution, this book is dedicated to you.

Furthermore, to all those American dissidents out there who feel there is no hope, or the silent complainers who yell at their televisions, or the rabble rousers who refuse to remain silent and accept the status quo, I want you to know I'm listening.

Now, Let's Turn Our Focus and Attention to What Is Needed from All of You

Never forget that the American people have all the power at their disposal to demand fundamental change. The problem is they are either afraid to use it, or just don't know exactly how. That's what this book intends to do.

The goal is to teach millions of Americans that they have all the power over their government and to show them how to use it effectively to minimize their size and power over the people. In addition, the focus will be on bold and unique ways to implement a new more liberty-based power structure in Washington, DC.

A realignment that, if fully implemented, would permanently alter the American people's relationship with their government by transferring power away from Washington, DC and back into the hands of the rightful owners of that power, We the People.

We have all heard the famous saying, "Rome was not built in a day." This is true; however, it is also important to note that Rome was not destroyed in a day either. It took years of excess, lawlessness, corruption, depravity, and violence to destroy the Roman Empire.

America, at this critical time and juncture, is reminiscent of the Roman Empire. Out of control corruption, unscrupulous politicians, gratuitous violence, and sexual depravity. This, and much more, took down the Roman Empire. How much further are we behind?

According to Alexander Fraser Tytler, a Scottish Professor and Historian, "A Democracy cannot exist as a permanent form of government. It can only exist until the voters discover that they can vote themselves largesse from the public treasury. From that moment on, the majority always votes for the candidates promising the most benefits."

According to Tytler, when this scenario eventually plays out, democracy collapses due to loose fiscal policy and massive corruption. This is also almost always followed by a dictatorship. In fact, Tytler even developed a political philosophy that shows the average age of the world's greatest civilizations typically only lasting around two hundred years.

According to Tytler's Eight Stages of a Democracy, All Civilizations Change in These Ways

1. From bondage to spiritual faith
2. From spiritual faith to great courage
3. From great courage to liberty
4. From liberty to abundance
5. From abundance to selfishness
6. From selfishness to apathy
7. From apathy to dependence
8. And from dependence back into bondage.[2]

At what stage do you presume America is at right now? We are forty-eight years over the average survival rate of the world's greatest civilizations. Some people might call that a victory. Others might say we got an extra forty-eight years over the average. Should we just be happy we made it this long and call it a bonus? Or should we continue to fight to defy Tytler's premonitions?

Well, if we compare the United States of America right now to that of the Roman Empire, it looks as though we should have at least another two hundred and fifty-two more years. Most historians calculate the total duration of the Roman Empire as lasting four hundred and ninety-nine years.

But please, have faith as I certainly do. Many other civilizations have lasted much longer. For instance, the Byzantine Empire lasted 1,123 years. The Silla Kingdom in the Korean peninsula lasted 992 years. Even the Ottoman Empire lasted about 600 years. We still have plenty of time to fix our country's problems and defy Tytler's eight stages of democracy.

Also, it is important to point out that we do not live in a democracy. We live in a constitutional republic. Lots of political pundits on television and radio like to call America a democracy. It is not. It is a constitutional republic. In a democracy you have mob rule without individual rights. In a constitutional republic, you do have individual rights.

Perhaps this is a reason those who govern us like to call America a democracy instead? Maybe they are trying to get us to forget that we do have individual rights? Remember, Benjamin Franklin did not tell Elizabeth Willing Powel, "It's a democracy if you can keep it."

If you needed any more proof that America is not a democracy, please feel free to recite the Pledge of Allegiance which states, "I pledge allegiance to the flag of the United States of America, and to the **Republic** for which it stands, one Nation under God, indivisible, with liberty and justice for all**."**

Franklin called it a republic and for good reason, one of which was the vested interest in our individual rights, which are enshrined in our Constitution. America's light of liberty still burns bright after two hundred and forty-eight years, however, the flame has gotten a little weaker. This is one flame we can never let be extinguished.

We will go back to the Gipper once again for this one. "Freedom is never more than one generation away from extinction. We don't pass it on to our children in the bloodstream. It must be fought for, protected, and handed on for them to do the same; or one day we will spend our sunset years telling our children and our children's children what it was once like in the United States when men were free."[3]

So, to those Americans who are still willing to fight for your freedoms, your liberties, and your country, please join me in this battle to preserve liberty by educating your family, your friends, your coworkers, and your communities. Be the change you want to see. Change the hearts and minds of those closest to you, and above all else, be focused and committed to fighting for these solutions. This is the type of book you will want to read with a yellow highlighter so you can refer back to the things you've learned.

The topics, the details, the documentation, the proof. What you are about to learn and discover about your elected officials, trusted scientists, members of Congress, political organizations, lobbyist groups, universities, laboratories, government agencies, presidents, and much more will shock you. In fact, after you finish reading this book, you will likely distrust your government even more than you probably already do.

Getting these proposals from concept to reality will not be easy. Many people are afraid of real fundamental change. However, if we all work together nothing is impossible. Remember, effective medicine is not supposed to taste like cherries and bubblegum; it is supposed to be bitter and nasty and hard to swallow, which is what makes it more effective.

So please join me, as I take you down a path of discovery, in which we will identify and expose the individuals, organizations, and policies that need to be defeated, defunded, or eliminated in order for all Americans to enjoy what Franklin and the Framers gifted to us; a republic if we can keep it.

CHAPTER ONE

Restoring Voter Confidence and Integrity

We must learn to identify our problems but only give power and energy to their solutions.

—Tony Robbins

It appears as if America has morphed into the hit song by the 1990s group REM; "It's the end of the world as we know it, and I feel fine." However, most of the American people I can assure you do not feel fine. If you are reading this now, you are likely part of that large group that is not feeling particularly too fine these days.

Most Americans are worried about their families, their futures, their children, and their safety and security. With crime rates skyrocketing all over the country, interest rates climbing higher, inflation at close to record numbers, and soaring gas prices, many Americans are being forced to make financial decisions they haven't had to make since the Great Depression.

Americans these days are feeling stressed out and stretched way too thin. Reminiscent of pre-war anxiety from the 1940s, Americans once again are genuinely scared for their future. Many are even stockpiling supplies such as generators, batteries, flashlights, transistor radios, emergency food, and plenty of weapons.

In fact, according to an April 2023 survey, 29 percent of the adult population, (that is seventy-four million Americans) self-identify as preppers. They are preparing for the unexpected in record numbers that have never been seen before.[1]

In this chapter, we are going to lay it all out on the line. We will discuss at length some uncomfortable truths about the last election. We will discuss different ways we can make our elections more secure. We will discuss some bold and brave solutions, and why they must be implemented to make sure what happened in the 2020 election never happens again.

Bold and brave, if not even radically pro-liberty-based solutions, are the only measures we must take to save our country and our elections. We will think outside the box and provide the kind of solutions that are guaranteed to upset those who believe that voter fraud doesn't exist, and the last election was the most secure in history.

There's No Voter Fraud, That's Just a Conspiracy

If Americans continue to lack the confidence in our elections and come to a consensus that their elections are no longer free nor fair, sadly, they will give up hope and abstain from exercising their constitutional right to vote. This is the exact strategy of our current government, which itself has some questions concerning its own legitimacy.

Through the use of intimidation, many Americans have unfortunately been on the receiving end of this government for daring to question their legitimacy and therefore their authority. Many people I know, including members of the last administration, have been targeted, arrested, and even indicted just for challenging the results of the last election.

They have endured such terrifying events such as middle of the night raids, politically motivated indictments, and illegal and unethical incarceration without representation. The current Department of Justice is using lawfare to target some Americans who dare to speak up and to silence and attack its political adversaries.

Elections Have Consequences

You've heard the saying, "You're entitled to your own opinions but not your own facts," right? It is typically said during political debates between candidates when someone is being called out for something they said. In today's world, they call it "having the receipts," meaning the proof to back it up.

For any of those out there who have ever heard of me before, or have seen my show and what I do, please note this is exactly how I live my life; with the truth always close to my heart. It is also another reason why I am writing this book.

According to the Heritage Foundation, there have been 1,499 confirmed cases of voter fraud across thirty-six different states. Of those cases, 1,275 have ended in a criminal conviction. This is proof that not only does voter fraud exist, but unfortunately it is also getting worse.[2]

In a recent Heartland/Rasmussen joint poll, **one out of five** voters who voted in the 2020 general election **admitted** to committing voter fraud through mail-in voting. This was not one out of a thousand. This was not one out of one hundred. This was not even one out of ten. This was one out of five!

Were These People Who Voted in the Election Even Eligible to Vote?

The Illegal Immigration Reform and Immigrant Responsibility Act of 1996. That title is about as long as the lie that illegal immigrants do not vote in our elections. I also find it ironic that the word "responsibility" is in the title in reference to people whose first act was to sneak in or be smuggled into our country, thus breaking the law.[3]

Even though the law strictly forbids noncitizens from voting in our federal elections, it does not restrict noncitizens from voting in smaller, more local elections such as city council, or school boards, or even in some cases, law enforcement positions, which to me, is mystifyingly and categorically insane.

Washington, DC for instance, our nation's national monument to insanity, allows noncitizens to vote in certain municipalities in local elections. The city of San Francisco, California allows noncitizens to vote on local school boards. Maryland and Vermont allow noncitizens to vote in municipal elections.

I started with Washington, DC, and I will end where the crazy begins. Washington, DC recently increased the insanity and passed a law that now allows noncitizens the right to vote in all non-federal elections. First it was local elections. Then it was municipalities, now it is state-level elections. Any guess as to what the final version will allow?

Most estimates show that between ten and as much as 13 percent of votes in every election, at every level, including federal, are cast by noncitizens. We need purple fingers with near impossible ink to get off.[4]

More Insanity

So now you might be asking yourself this question: What are these noncitizens using as identification to vote? Great question, glad you asked. How about state issued ID cards.

These nineteen states all issue driver's licenses and/or state identification documents.

1. California
2. Colorado
3. Connecticut
4. Delaware
5. Hawaii
6. Illinois
7. Maryland
8. Massachusetts
9. Minnesota
10. Nevada
11. New Jersey
12. New Mexico
13. New York
14. Oregon
15. Rhode Island
16. Utah
17. Vermont
18. Virginia
19. Washington, DC

What could possibly go wrong? I understand the safety reason argument but that is not my focus right now. They should not be issued any documentation at all because, well, they are illegal and should not be here in the first place, but that is a different matter.[5]

Back to the Poll Information

The poll, which was conducted in December 2023, asked 1,085 voters who voted by mail in the 2020 election a few simple questions that resulted in some shocking answers. The poll revealed that one in five participants admitted that they committed at least one form of voter fraud when they cast their ballots in that election.

When asked this question directly, "During the 2020 election, did you fill out a ballot, in part or in full, on behalf of a friend or family member, such as a spouse or a child?" Shockingly, 21 percent of respondents answered, "YES." (For those of you playing the home game, filling out or signing someone else's ballot is a violation of election law in every state with very few exceptions.

Parenthetically, another 17 percent in the same poll revealed that they voted in a state that they no longer lived in! It gets worse; yet another 17 percent also admitted to signing someone else's name on a ballot or envelope! (For those of you who are paying close attention, that is forgery, which is a serious crime.)

I guess if the FBI gets tired of spying on Americans, they could have a field day investigating this poll and its participants.[6]

Let's Unpack This Shall We?

According to a study, conducted by the United States Census Bureau, 155 million Americans voted in the 2020 election. In fact, the 2020 election had the highest participation rate of this century with 66.8 percent of eligible American voters taking part in it.

How can the United States Census Bureau even know that 66.8 percent of "eligible" voters voted in the last election, when nineteen states allow noncitizens the right to vote in our elections? It is this type of government doublespeak and lies that I have built my career on exposing.

The 2020 election had also the highest participation rate in history with regard to the use of voting by mail in any election, as 43 percent of all ballots cast were done so using this method. This is not a statistic our country should be proud of.

Voting by mail is not progress, it is an invitation to more fraud. This method of voting takes a sledgehammer to voter integrity measures and opens the floodgates for fictitious ballots. It also begs this question, how many of those 43 percent were even legal to vote in our elections?[7]

Tyranny Is Always Sold as Convenience

If at least 20 percent of voters have admitted to committing voter fraud. That's a potential thirty-one million fraudulent votes at a minimum that could have been cast in the last election! This is a number that without a doubt would meet the threshold for being outcome determinative.

Maybe it wasn't 20 percent. Maybe half of those who said they committed voter fraud were lying. Let's just say they were showing off or trying to impress the poll worker or someone else and only half were lying, and the other 10 percent were telling the truth.

If this is the case, that still leaves as many as 15,500,000 potentially fraudulent votes! Again, a large enough number to flip an election. But remember, the head of CISA and other agencies want us to believe that the 2020 election was the most secure in US history.

The Evil Practice of Ballot Harvesting

What is ballot harvesting? The practice of ballot harvesting takes place when someone other than the actual voter allows a third-party group or individual to collect absentee or mail-in ballots and drop them off at a polling station or precinct on the voter's behalf.

This practice became popular in the 2018 midterm elections—*the same year that our government created the Cyber Security and Infrastructure Security Agency (CISA), but I'm sure that's just a coincidence, too. More on CISA to come . . .*

Ballot harvesting is unfortunately legal in every state in America with varying degrees of laws and regulations. Historically, states would allow certain individuals, including campaign workers or even volunteers, to collect ballots from voters to mail or drop off at polling locations and election offices. This practice is wrought with fraud as there are very little safeguards in place to prevent voter fraud.

One of the major potentials for fraud in ballot harvesting is the chain of custody. The risk of these ballots being compromised increases dramatically when third-party distributors are used. Those risks include the potential for ballots to be filled-in by partisan volunteers or campaign officials, as well as manipulated or discarded completely.

Thankfully, since the aftermath of the 2020 election, many states have tightened up their rules on third parties being allowed to conduct ballot harvesting. Let me be clear, I am **not** a supporter of ballot harvesting.

I think this insidious practice should be banned in every state. There are already means for disabled, elderly, or terminally ill voters to cast their votes, so this practice is unwarranted, unfair, and unnecessary as well as prone to voter fraud. Unfortunately, it is still legal and corrupts our elections.

Making matters worse, different states now have different rules on who is or who is not permitted or eligible to drop off a voter's ballot. Some states, like Colorado, will let any voter drop off as many as ten ballots without so much as a signature affidavit!

Other states, like Arkansas, allow only the voter to drop off his or her own ballot with one exception: a legally designated bearer who is required to sign a signature affidavit on the envelope for authorization.

According to the 2024 updated version from Ballotpedia, which tracks and updates each state's rules and policies with regard to ballot harvesting, our system lacks a standard formality that allows bad actors to use these laws to commit voter fraud. Some states, as you will learn, take better precautions, but not all.

State-by-State Breakdown of Legal Guidelines for Ballot Harvesting

1. Alabama—very restrictive. Prohibits anyone other than the voter (except for immediate family) to return their ballot. Signature affidavit is required.
2. Alaska—somewhat lenient. Allows voters to have any person return their ballot, however, they must sign the envelope with a signature affidavit for authorization.

3. *Arizona*—restrictive. Prohibits anyone other than the voter (except for a family member, household member, or caregiver) to return their ballot. Signature affidavit is required.
4. Arkansas—very restrictive. Prohibits anyone other than the voter (except for a legally authorized designated bearer) to return a ballot; and a signature affidavit is required.
5. California—somewhat lenient. Law allows voters to permit any person to return their ballot, however, they require a signature affidavit for authorization.
6. Colorado—very lenient. Law allows any individual to collect up to ten ballots per election on behalf of any voters. Ballots must be returned within three days of the date noted on the envelopes, but no signature requirements!
7. Connecticut—somewhat restrictive. Law allows the voter to designate only a family member such as a spouse, parent, sibling, child, or grandchild. Does not specify signature affidavit requirements for authorization.
8. Delaware—more lenient. The law does not specify who can or cannot return a ballot on a voter's behalf.
9. Florida—restrictive. Prohibits anyone other than the voter (except for an immediate family member) to return no more than two ballots per. A signature affidavit is also required.
10. *Georgia*—somewhat restrictive. Prohibits anyone other than the voter (except for a family member or a caregiver) to return a ballot. However, they are not required by law to have a signature affidavit.
11. Hawaii—more lenient. The law does not specify who can or cannot return a ballot on a voter's behalf. Nor does it require a signature affidavit for authorization.
12. Idaho—more lenient. Law does not specify who can or cannot return a ballot on a voter's behalf, nor does it specify how many ballots are allowed per election to be dropped off. There is no signature affidavit requirement for authorization.
13. Illinois—more lenient. Law allows voters to permit any person to return their ballot without a signature affidavit requirement for authorization.

14. Indiana—restrictive. Prohibits anyone other than the voter (except for an immediate family member, household member, or attorney-in-fact) to return a ballot. Signature affidavit is required for authorization.

15. Iowa—somewhat restrictive. Prohibits anyone other than the voter (except for immediate family and household members) to return more than two ballots per election. However, there is no signature affidavit requirement for authorization.

16. Kansas—very lenient. Law allows voters to permit any person to return as many as ten ballots per election on voters' behalf without a signature affidavit requirement.

17. Kentucky—restrictive. Prohibits anyone other than the voter (except for immediate family members or a caregiver) to return a ballot. It also requires a voter assistant form to drop off a ballot but does not specify signature affidavit requirements for authorization.

18. Louisiana—restrictive. Prohibits anyone other than the voter (except for immediate family members) to return a ballot, and the designated person needs a signed affidavit for authorization from the secretary of state's office.

19. Maine—very lenient. Law allows voters to permit any person to return as many as five ballots on the voters' behalf without a signature affidavit requirement.

20. Maryland—more lenient. Law allows voters to permit any person to return their ballot on the voter's behalf without a signature affidavit requirement for authorization.

21. Massachusetts—somewhat restrictive. Prohibits anyone other than the voter (except for an immediate family member or caregiver) to return a ballot. However, no signature affidavit is required for authorization.

22. *Michigan*—somewhat lenient. Prohibits anyone other than the voter (except for an immediate family member, household member, or an election official) to return a ballot. However, there is no signature affidavit requirement for authorization.

23. Minnesota—restrictive. Law allows any person to return up to three ballots on voters' behalf per election. However, they require a signature affidavit and a notarized witness for authorization.

24. Mississippi—restrictive. Prohibits anyone other than the voter (except an immediate family member or election official) to return a ballot. However, there is a signature affidavit and notarized witness requirement for authorization.

25. Missouri—restrictive. Prohibits anyone other than the voter (except for immediate family members or relatives) to return a ballot. There is a notarized witness signature verification for authorization.

26. Montana—somewhat lenient. Prohibits anyone other than the voter (except for an immediate family member, household member, or caregiver) to return as many as six ballots per election on voters' behalf. However, there is no signature affidavit requirement for authorization.

27. Nebraska—more lenient. Allows a voter to appoint an agent to obtain and return their mail ballot. The law specifies that the agent may not be a candidate or member of a campaign committee unless they are a member of the voter's family. It also states that someone cannot serve as an agent for more than two voters.

28. *Nevada*—more lenient. The law does not specify who can or cannot return a ballot on a voter's behalf. There is also no signature affidavit requirement for authorization.

29. *New Hampshire*—very restrictive. Prohibits anyone other than the voter (except for immediate family members or a caregiver) to return a ballot. There is a notarized witness and a signature affidavit requirement for authorization.

30. New Jersey—somewhat lenient. An authorized messenger may return mail-in ballots for a voter. The messenger may not be a candidate and can return no more than three voters' ballots.

31. New Mexico—more lenient. Prohibits anyone other than the voter (except for an immediate family member or caregiver) to return a ballot. However, it does not specify how many ballots can be returned nor is there a signature affidavit requirement for authorization.

32. New York—more lenient. Does not specify how many or who can or cannot return ballots on voters' behalf nor is there a signature affidavit requirement.

33. North Carolina—restrictive. Prohibits anyone other than the voter (except near relatives such as spouse, parent, sibling, child, grandchild, in-laws, or stepchildren) to return a ballot. There is a notarized witness and a signature affidavit requirement for authorization.

34. North Dakota—more lenient. Does not specify who can or cannot return ballots or how many on voters' behalf, nor is there a signature affidavit requirement.

35. Ohio—somewhat restrictive. Prohibits anyone other than the voter (except for immediate and extended family members) to return a ballot. However, there are no signature affidavit requirements for authorization.

36. Oklahoma—restrictive. Prohibits anyone other than the voter (except an immediate family member or caregiver) to return a ballot. However, they will need to sign a notarized witness document for authorization.

37. Oregon—more lenient. Law allows voters to permit any person, even a campaign official, to return a ballot on a voter's behalf. There are no signature affidavit requirements for authorization.

38. *Pennsylvania*—restrictive. Prohibits anyone other than the voter (except for an immediate family member or a caregiver) to return a ballot. There is also a notarized witness signature affidavit required for authorization.

39. Rhode Island—restrictive. Prohibits anyone other than the voter (except for immediate family members and caregivers) to return their ballot, and there is a notarized witness signature affidavit requirement for authorization.

40. South Carolina—restrictive. Prohibits anyone other than the voter (except for immediate and extended family members and a caregiver) to return a ballot, and there is a signature affidavit requirement for authorization.

41. South Dakota—somewhat restrictive. The law does not specify who can or cannot return a ballot on a voter's behalf; however,

the designated returner needs to sign a signature affidavit for authorization.

42. Tennessee—more lenient. The law does not specify who can or cannot return a ballot on a voter's behalf, nor is there a signature affidavit requirement for authorization.

43. Texas—restrictive. Prohibits anyone other than the voter (except for immediate family members or a caregiver) to return a ballot and there is a signature affidavit requirement.

44. Utah—more lenient. The law does not specify who can or cannot return a ballot or even how many can be returned, nor is there a signature affidavit requirement.

45. Vermont—more lenient. The law does not specify who can or cannot return a ballot or even how many can be returned, nor is there a signature affidavit requirement.

46. Virginia—more lenient. The law does not specify who can or cannot return a ballot or even how many can be returned, nor is there a signature affidavit requirement.

47. Washington State—very lenient. Law allows voters to permit any person to return an unspecified number of ballots on voters' behalf without a signature affidavit requirement.

48. West Virginia—restrictive. Prohibits anyone other than the voter (except for immediate and extended family members and a caregiver) to return a ballot, and there is a signature affidavit requirement for authorization.

49. *Wisconsin*—restrictive. Prohibits anyone other than the voter (except for an immediate family member or a caregiver) to return a ballot. There is also a notarized witness signature affidavit required for authorization.

50. Wyoming—very lenient. Law allows voters to permit any person to return an unspecified number of ballots on voters' behalf without a signature affidavit requirement.

51. District of Columbia—more lenient. Law allows voters to permit any person to return their ballot without a signature affidavit requirement.[8]

So, you might be wondering, why did I list all fifty states and the District of Columbia's ballot harvesting rules and guidelines? Well, for one to show each state's vulnerabilities and strengths in regard to stopping mail-in ballot fraud.

In addition, they are listed for the reader to recognize the different loopholes in the laws and be spurred to try and get them changed or banned outright through statewide petitions and ballot initiatives.

Analysis of Ballot Harvesting Laws and Protocols

For the sake of time and to make my point, I decided to just highlight seven states that in the 2020 election had some type of issue such as voting irregularities, chain of custody problems, signature discrepancies, mandatory or voluntary recounts, or secretaries of state who unconstitutionally changed election laws and procedures without the legislatures' approval.

Those states are Arizona, Georgia, Michigan, Nevada, New Hampshire, Pennsylvania, and Wisconsin. All these states are swing states, and these seven states decided the last election with way more questions than answers. More states are considered swing states, but as was the case in 2020, it is likely these seven states will once again be the deciding factor on who wins the 2024 election.

Arizona, New Hampshire, Pennsylvania, and Wisconsin all have good restrictions in place to prevent ballot fraud and all require a signature affidavit requirement for authorization from the ballot carriers on the outside of each envelope.

Georgia and Michigan, two states which saw most problems of any states in the last election, have some restrictions on who can or cannot drop off a ballot on a voter's behalf; however, they do not require a signature affidavit on the envelope for authorization. Nevada does not even specify who can or cannot drop off ballots, and they do not require a signature affidavit from the carrier on the envelope for authorization.

As I stated previously, I am no fan of early voting, voting by mail, or ballot harvesting. All three of these practices should be banned outright or have severe restrictions put in place to ensure greater voter integrity and less likelihood of close elections being decided by fraud.

I encourage the readers to find their state in this list, and if you live in a state that does not have safety precautions and protocols in place to prevent ballot fraud, I highly implore you to take decisive action and start a petition to close those loopholes.

Facts, you know what they say, can be very stubborn things. Here are a few facts that have been well established, and there is record of in the form of either video, audio, or written documents.

In other words, these events all took place, and they are undisputable. In addition, many of these issues are centered around, you guessed it, mail-in ballots and ballot harvesting—the methods of choice for those who try to cheat in elections because they are the easiest methods available.

It is a fact that video surveillance caught Georgia election workers removing bins full of ballots from underneath tables. Whether they were used for nefarious purposes perhaps one day we will know. There are still way too many questions than there are answers.

It is a fact that voting machines are connected to the internet. Lots of politicians from both parties, as well as federal and state election officials, have gone out of their way to say that America's voting machines are never connected to the internet. As I stated previously, they are entitled to their own opinions but not their own facts.

According to a January 2020 NBC News article titled, "Online and Vulnerable": "Experts find nearly three dozen US voting systems connected to the Internet," a team of ten independent forensic and cybersecurity experts, who specialize in voting systems and elections, found over thirty-five voting systems were connected to the internet.[9]

Kevin Skoglund, a senior technical advisor at the Election Security Advocacy Group and the National Election Defense Coalition, noted that many of our voting machines are indeed plugged into the internet. Skoglund told NBC News, "We kept hearing from election officials that voting machines were never on the internet, but we know that isn't true."

It is a fact that poll workers in Michigan covered up the glass in the counting rooms. Their excuse, they say, for doing so was of course due to Covid restrictions and social distancing. They said the counting room was at full capacity, and they couldn't let anyone else in. But they still kept counting.

Counting votes as windows were covered in the rooms that were allegedly at capacity is a clear violation of election laws. Why didn't they stop counting? Why didn't they let people out, not cover the windows, and only resume counting when it was visible and challengeable?[10]

It is also a fact that many swing states unilaterally changed their election laws under the guise of Covid-19 protocols and without the consent of the state legislatures. This is a clear violation of the Elections Clause which states in Article One, Section Four, Clause One that, "the times, places, and manner of holding elections for Senators and Representatives, shall be prescribed in each state by the legislature thereof; but the Congress may at any time by Law make or alter such Regulations, except as to the choosing Senators." It does not say that a secretary of state can just unilaterally change election laws.

The United States Supreme Court has interpreted the Election Clause and even expanded its reach and responsibilities to include: enabling states "to provide a complete code for congressional elections," and the legislative oversight in addition to determining the "times and places; but also, in relation to notices, registrations,"[11] and protections and safeguards to prevent voter fraud, including conducting investigations.

Nowhere in the Constitution does it say in the Elections Clause or anywhere else for that matter, that a state level secretary of state can ignore the state legislature and decide on his or her own volition to change election laws without their consent. These new laws were unconstitutional and should never have been allowed.

The states that illegally changed election procedures should have forfeited that state's votes or reissued a new election after repealing the changes. There are literally hundreds more examples that I could list showing voting irregularities, but instead, we will let this last piece of evidence speak for itself.

We Did it!

You may remember an article from *Time* magazine written in early February 2021 that for all intents and purposes admitted that the election of 2020 was not legitimately decided. It was even titled, "The Secret History of the Shadowy Bipartisan Campaign That Saved the 2020 Election."[12] Why was this a secret, and what was the goal of this shadowy campaign? Who or what did it save? (I know, I know, there I go again, asking too many questions.)

However, if you read the article, you will find that they admit there were intelligence officials, both Democrat and Republican politicians, corporate CEOs, labor union representatives, and activist groups all working together to "save" the election.

This shadow group admits in the article that their work touched every aspect of the election. They even brag about forcing states to change voting procedures and election laws. They also bragged about how they secured hundreds of millions of dollars from private and public funding.

"This is the untold story of how thousands of activists in both parties accomplished the triumph of American democracy," said Norm Eisen, an attorney and former Obama administration official who was one of the masterminds behind the plan.[13]

So now that we have established that the 2020 election was clearly not "the most secure election in United States history," what can we do to make sure what happened last time never happens again?

Thankfully, some states have taken measures to make sure their elections are more secure. Over twenty-eight states have signed into law an outright ban or heavier restrictions on the private funding of our elections.

1. Alabama
2. Arizona
3. Arkansas
4. Florida
5. Georgia
6. Idaho
7. Indiana
8. Iowa
9. Kansas
10. Kentucky
11. Louisiana
12. Mississippi
13. Missouri
14. Montana
15. Nebraska
16. North Carolina

17. North Dakota
18. Ohio
19. Oklahoma
20. Pennsylvania
21. South Carolina
22. South Dakota
23. Tennessee
24. Texas
25. Utah
26. Virginia
27. West Virginia
28. Wisconsin[14]

Billionaires such as Meta/Facebook CEO Mark Zuckerberg found loopholes in election laws by donating $350 million to an organization called The Center for Technology and Civic Life. CTCL then distributed those funds, also known as "Zuckerbucks," to hundreds of counties across the country and to city election officials in forty-seven different states and the District of Columbia.

These grants were supposed to help with making sure Covid accommodations were paid for and implemented. In reality, the majority of the money went into the hands of election officials, county recorders, and Get Out the Vote operations.

According to the Capitol Research Center, Arizona was given over $5 million for their elections, Georgia was given $45 million, and Pennsylvania was given $25 million. All three of these states had contested and questionable elections.

Many states have also cleaned up their voter rolls and removed their states from participating in the Electronic Registration Information Center or the ERIC system. This system, which was supposed to be a bipartisan nonpolitical tool to clean up voter rolls, instead was a tool that was vulnerable to voter fraud.

So far, at least nine states have left the ERIC system. Those nine states are Missouri, Alabama, Florida, Iowa, Louisiana, Ohio, Texas, Virginia, and West Virginia.[15]

Moreover, eight additional states passed voter ID laws after the 2020 Election.

1. Arkansas
2. Idaho
3. Missouri
4. Montana
5. Nebraska
6. North Carolina
7. Ohio
8. Wyoming

They join Arizona, Georgia, Michigan, Nevada, North Carolina, Pennsylvania, and Wisconsin in joining the growing number of states that have passed photo identification requirements.[16]

This is a great start for sure, but there are a few other things we must do in order to further secure our elections:

One thing is for sure, we must all use **blue ink ballpoint pens** instead of felt tip black markers for filling out paper ballots. Some ballots actually say in the directions not to use these types of markers as they can bleed through and make it difficult for the voting machines to read.

When a voting machine can't identify who the vote was intended for, that ballot is typically placed in what is known as an adjudication file. These votes are then hand counted by election officials manually. This is where human error or nefarious behavior can influence our votes.

As I stated previously, if voters ever lose complete trust and faith in their elections, then they will likely retreat from voting and give continuous power to a small but tyrannical minority. Americans can never let this happen.

If this were to ever come to fruition, America would no longer be a free country. Instead, America would be ruled by a small but powerful tyrannical minority, with a goal of exerting total control over the people. Hundreds of thousands of Americans have fought and died to protect and preserve our freedoms and it is our duty to honor their sacrifices.

We can never allow our rights to be stripped away and taken from us and must use every resource possible at our disposal to protect them.

Preservation of our rights starts with the restoration of integrity, faith, and fairness in our elections.

That is why I am proposing five immediate fixes that would secure our elections, make them fairer for every voter, and of course, our number one goal, preserve liberty. In states in which the legislature is majority conservative, these five proposals should be introduced, passed, and signed into legislation as soon as possible. For those states that do not have a conservative majority legislature, these proposals could be more difficult to get signed into law but certainly not impossible.

So how do you get reforms passed when the legislature, secretary of state, or governor's office refuse to cooperate?

One way to accomplish this is by removing their ability to block the will of the voters by taking these proposals directly to the American people. State level ballot initiatives can be quite an effective tool to bypass uncooperative legislatures and allow the people to decide directly. If these proposed changes can't get done legislatively, then each proposal should be introduced to voters directly through ballot initiatives in each respective state.

Remember, out of the twenty-eight states that have banned the private funding of our elections, four states whose governors issued a veto were overridden by the state legislatures. Even more fantastic was that two states, Louisiana and Wisconsin, got around the roadblocks from their governor's office and the state legislature by bypassing them and going straight to the decision-makers. We know them as voters.

In both states, the people decided, and they determined they didn't want private billionaires funding their elections. How amazing would it be to see this type of ban in the rest of the states?

Five Proposed Changes Needed to Secure Our Elections

1. Legislation or ballot initiatives in states that still do not have voter ID laws. Every state should have a mandatory voter ID with a clear and current photo and current address. (This must also match the voter file and signature card on record.)
2. Legislation or ballot initiatives to vote on removing voting machines and going back to counting votes in smaller precincts on paper

ballots. The machines are faulty, can be hacked or manipulated, and are plugged into the internet. It worked much better with paper ballots hand counted in smaller precincts.

3. Legislation or ballot initiative to eliminate mail-in voting (except for the military abroad and disabled voters) and permanently ban ballot harvesting in every state, with very few exceptions. There is nothing fair or necessary about gathering up votes and no-fault mail in voting. The longer the voting cycle, the more time there is for potential fraud. If we are going to restore integrity and put faith back in our elections, mail-in voting and ballot harvesting must become a thing of the past.

4. Legislation or ballot initiative to require voters to be registered to vote no less than thirty days before an election. One of the scams some states are deploying is same day registration on election day. This would help eliminate illegal voting in multiple states which is another form of voter fraud.

5. Legislation or ballot initiative that demands all ballots must be counted on election night in the county where the votes were cast, and by midnight on election night. No exceptions. Also, all results must be given simultaneously to prevent "sandbagging" of votes by certain counties that like to wait for others to report first.

The bottom line is that it should be easy to vote but impossible to cheat. Having photo ID requirements does not "disenfranchise" anyone. You need an ID to withdraw money from the bank. You need an ID to drink alcohol. You need an ID to rent a car. You need an ID to drive a car. But you don't need an ID to vote?

There are many other steps Americans must take but the biggest one is taking initiative. Change starts at the local level. Once you can exact change, you are no longer fearful or powerless. The more Americans that get involved in their local elections, the more eyeballs there are on election officials. When someone knows they are being watched or monitored they are less likely to do something that will get them in trouble.

Our number one goal is to keep those that administer our elections honest. The best way to achieve this is by letting them know that this time around, we will be watching everything much more closely.

We will need to closely watch the ballot counters at the counting centers. We will need to watch the drop box locations, especially late at night. We will need to watch the precincts and all the polling stations, including the parking lots. We need to make sure that vans or buses with out of state plates are not dropping off tons of people to vote or that boxes of ballots are being delivered in the middle of the night.

Remember, if something just doesn't seem right it usually is not. Always be on the lookout for anything that seems to be out of place, because most of the time your instincts are correct. Lastly, be alert, be ready, and always go vote.

The right to a free and fair election is the bedrock of our Republic. Enshrined in our Constitution is this right to vote and choose our representatives. It is also what sets us apart from so many different countries around the world who do not have the freedom or right to choose their leaders. The right to pick and choose those who will represent you every two to four years must always remain a free and fair exercise.

When the American people feel as though their elected leaders, who are supposed to be guardians of their freedoms, no longer serve the will of the people, it is time to change out those leaders for new ones. That is why our system and form of government allows for checks and balances.

In a free society, fair elections are the great equalizer. They allow us to fire certain politicians and reward others for doing a good job. They also allow us to bring in new leadership when the old ones get stale.

Many politicians like to say they went to Washington, DC to change the system, however, over time Washington, DC changed them. Without the right to vote these politicians out of office, we will no longer be governed by those who represent us, but rather by those who represent themselves.

As Thomas Jefferson once famously said, "When the government fears the people there is liberty. When the people fear their government there is tyranny." Do we want to live in a society where the people fear their government, or the government fears the people?

I know my answer.

CHAPTER TWO

Unintended Consequences
of Big Government

Ever since the 2000 election between George W. Bush and Al Gore and the subsequent outcome, our elections have been marred with controversy. From the hanging chads in Florida, to the 537-vote recount squeaker that eventually put George W. Bush in the White House, the start of the new century was very eventful. The new century brought with it new hope and a fresh start, but it also brought turmoil. Above all else, it showed how divided the country had become, at least temporarily.

However, the division millions of Americans felt would soon be forgotten. What happened on September 11, 2001, brought the American people together like no other time in our history since the end of World War II. The tragedy of 9/11 is what united us and reminded us that at our core we are all still Americans.

September 11, 2001, is a day that will live in infamy forever. It was a day unlike any other day America had experienced since maybe the assassination of President John F. Kennedy. Most older Americans who lived through that terrible event can recollect exactly where they were and what they were doing on that fateful day.

After the devastating events of 9/11 unfolded in New York City, the Pentagon, and Shanksville, Pennsylvania, the country experienced an incredible amount of pride and patriotism. It appeared as if every American was wearing patriotic clothing and waving American flags. Sadly, it took such a tragic event to bring Americans closer together; however, the patriotic love fest was very short-lived.

Just one month later, Americans were given a new focus to help them stay angry and divided when George W. Bush's administration, with the political winds at their back, along with the help of the war hawking neo-cons from both parties, decided it was time to declare war and send our men and women into the mountains of Afghanistan.

This started what would go down into the annals of history as the longest confrontation and military operation in United States history. A few years later, while still in Afghanistan, George W. Bush's administration decided to declare war against Saddam Hussein and the country of Iraq. So now we had two wars being fought simultaneously. What could possibly go wrong?

As former Chicago Mayor Rahm Emmanuel once famously said, "Never let a good crisis go to waste." Politicians like Rahm Emmanuel prey on scared Americans by exploiting their fears in order to grow the federal government.

Remember, it is both parties that voted to invade our privacy. Never forget it was George W. Bush's administration, who lobbied for and helped sign into law "The Patriot Act," which allows for the targeting of Americans and increased spying under the guise of fighting terrorism.

In addition to the misnamed Patriot Act came the creation of The Department of Homeland Security. With over 240,000 employees, it is the third largest department of the federal government. Nothing like Big Government to the rescue to keep us all safe. This gigantic arm of our intelligence apparatus is a shining example of why you never look to the government to solve a problem.

Inside the Department of Homeland Security now sits:

1. U.S. Customs and Border Protection (CBP)
2. U.S. Immigration and Customs Enforcement (ICE)
3. Transportation Security Administration (TSA)
4. Federal Emergency Management Agency (FEMA)
5. U.S. Secret Service (USSS)
6. U.S. Coast Guard (USCG)

7. Countering Weapons of Mass Destruction (CWMD)
8. Office of Intelligence and Analysis (I&A)
9. Office of the Inspector General (OIG)
10. And the office of Cybersecurity and Infrastructure Security Agency, which I will touch on soon.

It is often said that history is littered with good intentions that have gone horribly wrong. Perhaps the Bush administration and the Republican-controlled House and Senate at that time were caught up in the moment of "let's get those darn terrorists"—but obviously didn't think it through or at least weigh it against the Constitution.

They didn't ask these fundamental questions: Is this necessary? What will the Department of Homeland Security look like in five or ten years? Most importantly, will the Department of Homeland Security live up to its namesake and provide our homeland with security?

Judging by the current secretary, we can see that DHS is about the furthest thing removed from protecting our homeland; however, we will leave illegal immigration and border security issues for another chapter.

Along with all the changes in so-called safeguards for the American people came another tool, since 2002, that was the unofficial start of the federalization of our elections. I am referring to the Help America Vote Act also known as HAVA.

After the 2000 election, the hysteria in and around Washington, DC reached a fever pitch. However, once the constant talk and chatter from both the media and the politicians about "pregnant chads" and "hanging chads" tempered down, our government stepped in, and in their brilliant ways and infinite wisdom, decided to save us from ourselves.

Many politicians saw an opportunity to take advantage of what transpired in Florida in the year 2000 and decided for political reasons that the states could no longer administer their own elections, and therefore, the government must step in to help.

The worst thing you could ever hear from the government is, "I'm from the government and I'm here to help." However, that is exactly what happened. Our brilliant politicians decided to step in and "fix" the problem.

The American people need to look within themselves for the answers to fix their problems, not the federal government. All the federal government does is create more problems; and typically, at the expense of our freedoms.

"Knock knock." "Who's there?" "It's me again." "Me again who?" "Me, Mr. Government, and I'm here to federalize, sorry, I meant to fix our elections." And that is exactly what happened next. George W. Bush's administration, along with an all too eager Republican House and Senate, decided to plant the first seeds towards federalizing our elections.

For the sake of honesty and accuracy, which I hold to the utmost importance, HAVA does not technically federalize our elections, but it does provide **federal** funds to states to "modernize their voting equipment."

Let me translate this for you. Here are some federal dollars to spread around so you can buy brand new hackable voting machines so we can make sure we have the most secure elections in US history, right CISA?

HAVA was designed to improve the administration of elections in the United States. Let's stop right there. The administration of elections? Don't the states administer and oversee the elections? Do you see what happened here folks?

The 2000 election had a few minor issues, so of course the federal government saw an opportunity to overstep its boundaries and try to force states to take federal money and purchase voting machines.

It is not mandatory, but if a state wants these funds, it needs to modernize its elections—thus, the dangling of the famous carrot of government grants, earmarks, and allocations. In addition to receiving federal money to buy hackable voting machines, HAVA changed our elections by creating the Election Assistance Commission, which is basically the equivalent of the HAVA police. The EAC is tasked with paying states to strictly adhere to HAVA'S guidelines by adopting voting system protocols whereby each state must adhere to federally mandated election rules. This sounds an awful lot, like the states are no longer free to administer their elections as is written in the Constitution.

I am a big believer in the best government is the smallest government. In fact, I would say that for the government to be working effectively it must be as inconsequential in all our lives as humanly possible. Each state has the right to conduct its elections based on the Elections Clause and nowhere does it say anything about the federal government conducting our elections.

Our elections should be 100 percent administered as the United States Constitution says they should be, at the hands of our state legislatures. We should repeal the Help America Vote Act because it is unconstitutional.

We should also ban unreliable and easily hackable voting machines. In addition, we should also go back to administering all our elections through paper ballots, hand counted in smaller precincts, with the result guaranteed before midnight on election night.

Just because we have the technology to vote electronically, doesn't mean we should. As I often say, tyranny is frequently sold as convenience. In order to have more honest elections, we should keep hackable technology out of them.

The Most Secure Election in United States History

You may have noticed a few subtle digs at the Cybersecurity and Infrastructure Security Agency. Founded in November of 2018, CISA's primary functions were to enhance the security, resilience, and reliability of our nation's cybersecurity and intelligence infrastructure.

CISA is mainly responsible for the oversight of:

1. Mitigating vulnerabilities in our critical infrastructure
2. Stopping cyber-attacks in progress and identifying the sources.

It should come as a shock to no one that CISA admits that they share their intelligence with all our intelligence agencies. Instead of solely concentrating on cybersecurity and infrastructure, CISA has had a major focus on policing social media. By 2020, CISA would routinely report posts deemed "misinformation," and by 2021, CISA opened its own Office of Disinformation.

However, as sizzling as that information may be, here is the full steak. Independent investigative journalist Yehuda Miller discovered through a Freedom of Information Act (FOIA) request supplied by CISA that the agency was conducting secret meetings, organized by CISA officials, including at 3:30 p.m. Eastern time on November 3, 2020, which was election day.[1]

Moreover, this meeting was with CISA, and as many as two hundred additional partners consisting of: private individuals, government agencies, private businesses, corporate CEOs, and media outlets.

What was even more concerning were the election-related companies also in attendance such as: Scytl, Dominion, ES&S, ERIC Systems, Runbeck, Microsoft, Amazon, and several secretaries of state offices.

So why would CISA be organizing secret meetings towards the late afternoon on election day with government agencies including voting machine companies Scytl, Dominion, ES&S, Big Tech companies like Amazon and Microsoft, and about a half dozen secretaries of states?

What were these meetings about? Why did they feel it was necessary to hide them from the public? Why did it take a FOIA request to find out about them taking place? Also, here's a fun fact, did you know Chris Krebs, the former director of CISA, and Alex Stamos, the former Facebook security officer went into the consulting business together?[2]

One of the Krebs-Stamos Group's biggest accounts was SolarWinds. You may remember hearing about SolarWinds back in September 2019. The SolarWinds Corporation had numerous versions of its network management software installed in many of our government's critical infrastructure.

Hackers were able to breach the systems and access the main network. Once inside, they were able to release malicious software into at least eighteen thousand private or public companies as well as thirty-seven defense industry–based organizations. The SolarWinds attack was one of the worst cyber-attacks in our history.

Now the company has hired Chris Krebs, and he is overseeing the critical infrastructure of SolarWinds Corporation; One must wonder, when will he announce that SolarWinds is now the most secure company in US history?

In 2021, CISA created the Cybersecurity Advisory Committee, and although some members of this new committee came from the security world, many did not. There were mayors, politicians, CEOs, lawyers, university presidents, even a retired professional women's basketball player.

However, the most shocking name on the committee list was former Twitter attorney and chief information officer Vijaya Gadde. Gadde, you may remember, was grilled on Capitol Hill for her role in Twitter's shadow banning and censorship controversies. Gadde was behind the decision to censor the Hunter Biden laptop story, which turned out to be 100 percent true.

She was also behind the banning of several high-profile Twitter accounts, including President Trump's. In 2019, she convinced then Twitter CEO Jack Dorsey not to sell political advertisements during the 2020 presidential election. Many have said the reason was due to President Trump's massive following on the platform. A few years later, she permanently banned President Trump from the platform.

So, let's recap: once again Republicans introduced and signed into law yet another level of federalization of our elections. And again, the government agency created may have been for good intentions, but just like the Department of Homeland Security, turned its focus and attention onto something else.

Balancing the Electorate: Metropolitan, Micropolitan, and Sparsely Populated

Sometimes the good Lord works in mysterious ways. When I started writing this book, this part of this chapter was not in the news cycle. In April 2024, Charlie Kirk, media figure and founder of Turning Point USA, a youth organization that promotes conservative principles at colleges and universities around the country, decided to lead a movement to get the state of Nebraska to switch to a "winner take all" electoral model as forty-eight other states currently follow.[3]

Charlie may be worried that part of the state might not vote for President Trump, and he might need the extra vote to win a close election. Nebraska is doing things right. In fact, every state should follow Nebraska's and Maine's lead in allocating electoral votes by counties.

Let's Have Fifty Nebraskas

There are a total of 3,142 counties or county equivalents in the United States of America. These consist of forty-one independent cities, parishes, boroughs, municipalities, incorporated areas, and the District of Columbia.[4]

An incredible 50 percent of the entire US population lives in only one hundred and forty-four of these counties! In addition, of the top twenty-five most populated counties in America, seventeen of them are in what are considered blue states, while three are in what are considered swing states, and another five are in what are considered red states.[5]

page

So, what does this mean? This means that the other 50 percent of the entire United States population lives in the other 2,998 counties. Talk about a disparity! This means that less than 5 percent of the entire population makes most of the important decisions for the other 95 percent!

Therefore, if you are one of those Americans who choose to live in the less populated counties of your state, just outside of the hustle and bustle of the big city, sadly in our current system you have no real voice, no real say, and quite frankly no real vote on who your federal level elected officials will be.

Don't you think it's way past time that every vote should be counted in a more balanced and fair way? Can we really continue to label ourselves a "fully representative government" of the people, by the people, and for the people if 95 percent of Americans have no real representation? This disparity is based on population not fairness. Perhaps we can change that.

How We Can Make All Votes Count for All Americans

The majority of the United States of America's fifty states are mostly red states with big blue cities. One simple way to prove this is just look at any presidential map in the last hundred years and you can clearly see there is way more red than blue.

But what gives many red states the blues is their sprawling urban cities. Take Colorado as an example: Most of the state is red except for the Denver metropolitan area. Take Denver's vote and break it down by county, and it is clear how the vicious cycle of no representation continues.

Another example would be the state of Nevada. The Silver State is as red as can be once you travel outside of Clark County. Even a supposedly blue state like Illinois is probably more red than blue if you remove the power structure of Cooke County.

But how do these states typically vote in just about every election? They typically go to the Democratic Party due to the heavy urban population centers that drown out the votes of the rest of the state.

So, to all those millions of red-blooded Americans out there who are trapped in blue states and feel like strangers, this was designed with you in mind. The bigger the cities grow, the more isolated the 95 percent of Americans feel. What if all the votes that are currently being marginalized and discounted as "fly-over country" suddenly had their votes count even half as much as they do now?

First off, these voters are more than just tiny dots flying overhead in an airplane. They are our farmers, our ranchers, our hunters, and our fishermen. They are the lifeblood of our economy and of vital importance to our health and well-being. They are the Americans who live in the heartland of this great country.

These irreplaceable and important people should be admired and respected for the hard labor-intensive work that they do. Americans who choose to cultivate our land and work on our farms sacrifice so much for the rest of the country.

Far too often than not, their enormous daily sacrifices often sadly go unnoticed. Let's face it, farmers, ranchers, hunters, and fishermen are far more noble professions than lawyers, judges, politicians, and lobbyists.

Just imagine for a moment how better off America would be if our farmers, ranchers, hunters, and fishermen had political power equal to that of lawyers, judges, politicians, and lobbyists? America would be much better off for it and quickly would start to resemble once again what America has always been, which is a center right constitutional republic.

What if we changed the Electoral College to represent all the people in each respective state rather than just those in the big cities? What if these smaller counties across the country, which currently have virtually no say in who they choose to represent them, suddenly did? What if they were given more power at the expense of the top one hundred and forty-four counties?

Here's How This Plan Would Work

As mentioned previously, in all but two states, the electoral votes are decided on a "winner takes all" basis. Nebraska and Maine instead award some of their electoral votes by regions or counties.

What if instead of going with the "winner takes all" model in the rest of the forty-eight states, we followed Nebraska and Maine's model and, in every state, counted electoral votes based on population in each county rather than the popular vote of each state?

The United States of America's 3,142 counties are divided into three different population sizes. These counties are categorized as metropolitan areas, micropolitan areas, and sparsely populated or uninhabited areas. Okay, now let's do a little math.

1. **Metropolitan** counties consist of a population of **50,000 or more** people. These are typically the largest counties in each state.
2. **Micropolitan** counties have a population of **at least 10,000** people but not more than **49,999**. These are typically smaller communities outside of the nearest large city.
3. **Sparsely populated** counties, or county equivalents are where as few as a handful of people live, to as many as **9,999** inhabitants. These are where most of the roads are unpaved, homes are built in the middle of nowhere, typically within a few miles of one another, or in once vibrant areas that have been left abandoned as ghost towns.

Of the **3,142** total counties, **998** are in metropolitan counties, **1,408** are in micropolitan counties, and another **736** are in sparsely populated counties.[6]

What if each one of the 3,142 total counties in America were awarded at least one electoral vote?

Most organizations and individuals who bring up changing the Electoral College advocate for its abolishment. This would be a grave mistake and would allow heavily populated states like California and New York to run up the popular vote totals and declare one candidate the winner based on an unfair and fundamentally flawed system. Here's a better solution to give everyone's vote, regardless of where in a state they live, the same weight.

It Would Break Down Like This

In this new and more appropriate model, metropolitan counties would be awarded **four** electoral votes based on the size of the population. Most big cities have double the population of the rest of the state, so we must be fair.

Next, we will award micropolitan counties with **two** electoral votes, again based on population.

Finally, sparsely populated counties would receive **one** electoral vote. Just because these Americans choose to live outside of the big cities, doesn't mean their voices should not count.

Okay, here is where it gets a little more complicated, but if you follow right along it is easy to understand.

The total number of electoral votes that could be awarded based on a four, two, and one distribution rate for all of America's 3,142 counties would be 7,545. In order to win the election, a candidate would need to achieve at least 51 percent or more of the 7,545 total possible votes. This would mean the winner would need at least 3,847 (51 percent) of the 7,545 total votes to win.

Sounds complicated? It's not. This model, if ever fully adopted, would give the American people back their power and return our country back to the constitutional republic it was intended to be.

In addition, this model would finally allow for true independent voices and voters to be heard. Also, these types of candidates running for office would finally be able to compete in statewide elections.

This model is designed to turn on its head the two-party duopoly monster by stripping power away from both major parties and making it more fair for independent candidates to compete and win elections.

Republicans typically win most counties in America, so this model will allow more third parties and Independents the opportunity to compete more fairly and win more of America's counties.

This new system, if ever fully implemented, would give a voice to the voiceless and make their vote count more equally. No longer will the forgotten be left out in the cold or feel silenced. This system is designed to remove the power structure from the big cities and transfer it back to We the People who won't abuse it.

According to the Associated Press, in 2016 President Trump won 2,626 counties to Hillary Clinton's 487. Also, in the 2020 presidential election, President Trump won 2,588 counties to Joe Biden's 551.[7, 8]

With Republicans already winning most counties in the United States of America, this model is designed as a leg up for the independent voter and candidates to compete for more counties.

In our current system, Independent candidates do not typically even have a chance to compete and win elections. Independent candidates in our current model serve mainly two purposes: they either act as a spoiler against one party or the other, or they serve as a protest vote when the top two parties' candidates are too unpopular.

In this new model, Independent voters will no longer feel as though they are throwing their vote away or helping another candidate. This also allows for Independent candidates to compete for and win many more of our country's 3,142 counties.

We like to say that we live in a constitutional republic with individual rights. The reality is we have been run for far too long by an entrenched mob of power hungry and unscrupulous politicians hellbent on controlling our every move. It is time to take back our power by taking away theirs.

This is how you give the power back to the American people. This is how you defeat the influence and vote advantage of the big metropolitan cities, and this is how you release the stranglehold these big cities have had over each state and the country for far too long.

Remember, my goal is to come up with different outside-the-box solutions to preserve our liberties. I understand many people reading this might not agree with my solution. That's okay, because the truth is I am not trying to win a popularity contest here, I'm trying to save our country.

In fact, one of my quotes from *A-to-Z Quotes* fits best right here: "I would rather be loved by millions and hated by the same number rather than moderately liked by everyone."[9]

It seems these days, due to censorship and political correctness, many media figures are too afraid to speak their mind and take bold and brave and even unpopular decisions. They are too concerned with the next promotion or job and would rather be universally liked and accepted by everyone. I am not one of them.

CHAPTER THREE

Closing Our Borders

Our Founding Fathers and originalist judges fundamentally understood the incredible importance of having our nation's borders secure. In 1833, Joseph Story, an associate justice of the United States Supreme Court, stated this about immigration policy, "If aliens might be admitted indiscriminately to enjoy all the rights of legal citizens, at the will of a single state, the Union itself might be endangered by an influx of foreigners, hostile to its institutions, ignorant of its laws and powers, and incapable of a due estimate of its privileges."[1]

Joseph Story was correct. Also, immigration without assimilation is an invasion as well as a recipe for disaster. Almost every country of the world has strong laws in regard to immigration enforcement, as well as guidelines for assimilation, including a requirement to be working and/or speaking the language.

For instance, Mexico, our neighbor to the south, has strict immigration enforcement laws to protect their borders with Guatemala and other border countries. This includes deploying their National Guard to stop cross-border invasions. The Mexican government clearly understands the importance of border security, why don't we?

How is this for irony? It is a felony under Mexican Law under Article 123 of the General Law of Population that mandates a penalty of up to two years in prison if you are found to be living or entering the country illegally.

Moreover, Article 118 of the General Law of Population states that any foreigner, who has previously been deported, or caught trying to reenter the country illegally, will be guilty of another more severe felony that is punishable by up to ten years in prison.

Oh, the irony!

In America, not only are you less likely to even be deported, but if you are caught trying to reenter America, no matter how many times, you will likely be rewarded with identification cards, drivers licenses, welfare in some cases, free food, free shelter, free education, and free health care. To say our system is broken is an understatement, it's practically nonexistent.[2]

There Are Only Eleven Million Illegal Aliens Living in the Shadows

These immigration lies, which have been told since at least the 1990s, are like the fisherman who catches a minnow but tells you it was a shark. There are not eleven million illegal aliens hiding or living in the shadows, afraid to show their faces and participate in our society. If you believe this tall tale, I have some incredible oceanfront property to sell you in Arizona.

In the 1990s, it is true that there were approximately eleven million illegal aliens living in the shadows. However, by the early 2000s, that number doubled to twenty-two million. It is safe to say that many years later, under the constant assault of invasion, the number of illegal aliens in this country is a lot higher than twenty-two million.

According to USAfacts.org at least ten million illegal aliens have been encountered at the US southern border from October 2019 until January 2024. To give you an idea of how many individuals that is, the entire state of Michigan's population is at least ten million people.

That means we have allowed the equivalent of the entire state of Michigan's population into our country as illegal immigrants! Based on these numbers alone, clearly there are at least thirty-two million illegal aliens in the United States of America.[3]

But these lies keep getting exposed and the number of illegal aliens in our country continues to grow larger. According to a March 2024 report from MigrationPolicy.Org, in 2022, there were 46.2 million illegal aliens in the United States of America. However, with the recent and continuous purposeful surges of illegal aliens at our southern border, the 46.2 million number, being two years outdated, is also likely wrong too.

According to the Federation for American Immigration Reform (FAIR), 2023 marked the highest level of illegal immigration in US history! How bad is the problem? According to Customs and Border Protection's end of the year statistics, the CBP has encountered over 3.2 million illegal aliens at our southern border.[4]

That is more than all four years of the Trump administration combined! The fiscal year total of 2023 was 16 percent higher than it was in fiscal year 2022, which saw at least 2.76 million, and an incredible 63 percent increase over fiscal year 2021!

The Women and Children Farce

Most open borders advocates claim many of these border crossers are arriving with their families. They say they are just looking for a better life here in America. However, this is not the case. In fact, 65 percent or 2.06 million of 2023's 3.2 million encounters were single adults traveling with no children!

Other Consequences of Open Borders

It is not just illegal immigration that is the problem. Other factors are the by-products and consequences of open borders, such as: strain on our financial resources, job losses, increased homelessness, and more welfare recipients. There is also the enormous challenge of educating children in overcrowded schools whose native language is not English.

In addition, statistics show that higher levels of illegal immigration have a direct correlation to higher crime rates, drug abuse, diseases, public health risks, and violent crimes such as abductions and human trafficking.

Fentanyl Deaths Are Skyrocketing

According to a recent study by the CDC, fentanyl deaths are skyrocketing all across the country. Over 110,000 drug overdoses have occurred in 2023, and 71 percent were caused by fentanyl! If the borders are not closed, and the fentanyl keeps pouring in, some projections forecast upwards of two hundred thousand Americans could die as a result of fentanyl poisoning by 2025.[5]

Think of how many people's lives have been snuffed out and will continue to be. How many hopes and dreams will have been shattered? How many countless loved ones will be left behind to pick up the pieces? Drug overdoses do not just kill the individual, they also destroy the lives of the families and loved ones who are never the same after such a loss.

This powerful and lethal drug must be stopped from entering into our country. Losing so many lives is not just a travesty, it could become a national security risk as well. Long-term deadly fentanyl shipments, coupled with endless open borders, is the recipe for national suicide.

So, How Many Illegal Aliens Are Here Now?

Well, according to a Center of Immigration study dated March 2024, and analysis from the Census Bureau's current population survey, America's foreign-born population is now at 51.4 million. This number represents about 15 percent of the entire population. This percentage is greater or equal to the total population of at least thirty-three states![6]

The Great Replacement Theory Is Real and Happening

Many political pundits and open borders advocates call "the great replacement theory" a conspiracy or xenophobic talking point. They point out and label anyone who dares to prove they are lying as anti-immigrant or racist. However, the data suggests that not only is the great replacement theory real, but it is happening every day right before our eyes.

According to additional information pertaining to the statistics of the United States of America's foreign-born populations, studies show that the foreign-born immigration population has nearly tripled since 1970. By the 1990s, the rate nearly doubled from the 1970s and is up an additional 40 percent since just the turn of the century.

Due to America's current open border policies, statistics show that the foreign-born population in America has grown in record numbers since Joe Biden took office, tripling that of President Trump and even doubling that of Barack Obama.

At 172,000 minimum encounters per month, the average increase in America's foreign-born population under Biden is four times higher than it was under President Trump. If these current trends continue or increase, experts predict the foreign-born population will likely eclipse over 60 million by 2028.

This current administration is not making things any better either, as they have issued 296 executive orders directed towards immigration policy. For the sake of time, I will not list them all; however, I will point out some of the more egregious and purposeful acts that directly exacerbated our problems.

It is also important to note that most of these executive orders were all issued within the first one hundred days of this administration or by the end of the first year. Here are some of the Biden administration executive orders that demonstrate their complete disregard for the American people's safety and security.

1. January 21, 2021, his first day in office, Biden terminated the National Emergency declaration at the southern border (Proclamation 9844) thereby immediately stopping all construction of the southern border wall.
2. Also on January 21, 2021, the new Biden regime gave the green light to illegal aliens everywhere by refortifying the unlawful and unconstitutional Deferred Action for Childhood Arrivals, also known as DACA. With this action, Biden directed the Department of Homeland Security (DHS) in concert with the attorney general of the United States to cease arrests or deportations.
3. Again, on day one, Biden signed the United States Citizenship Act, giving blanket amnesty to millions of new illegal immigrants and signaling to other potential new arrivals that America's borders are wide open without the threat of deportation.
4. On February 2, 2021, Biden signed Executive Order 14010, which repealed the Trump-era "Remain in Mexico" rule. This order allowed those seeking asylum to remain here in the United States rather than in Mexico during their processing.
5. Also in February 2021, the Biden administration upended Title 42 requirements by allowing unaccompanied minors without parents to stay here illegally and without penalty or fear from deportation.

6. On March 10, 2021, the Biden administration announced the reinstatement of the CAM program, an Obama-era parole program that allowed for illegal aliens to bypass family-based immigration laws adopted by Congress. This rule gave individuals already here illegally not just the right to stay, but even more egregious, the right to use chain migration from sponsored countries such as El Salvador, Guatemala, and Honduras.

7. On March 31, 2021, Biden's Department of Health and Human Services (HHS) through the Office of Refugee Resettlement (ORR) issued new rules that rolled back requirements for criminal background checks on adults who sponsor unaccompanied minors inside the United States. These background checks would have prevented child predators, traffickers, and violent criminals with records from sponsoring these children.

8. On September 30, 2021, DHS Secretary Mayorkas issued a memorandum stating, "just because someone is here illegally doesn't mean that should be a deportable offense," thus creating a backdoor amnesty program fueled by the discretion of prosecutors to decide whether some individuals should be deported.

9. On October 12, 2021, DHS effectively suspended large scale worksite enforcement. This move basically erased the E-Verify program by allowing employers to hire illegal aliens without any repercussions.

10. In November 2021, the Biden administration created a program called ATD, or Alternatives to Detention, thus establishing the "catch and release" program. These programs forced law enforcement, Immigration and Customs Enforcement (ICE), and the United States Border Patrol to release hundreds of thousands of illegal aliens into the United States interior. In 2022 alone, over 338 thousand illegal aliens were released through this program.[7]

That was just what the Biden administration did in the first one hundred days of its first year alone! Since this time, our immigration system, of which there is none, has only gotten considerably worse.

By March 2023, the Biden administration was directing ICE to continue to ignore the need for deportations, allowing as many as 5.3 million illegal immigrants to stay in America indefinitely, including over 400,000 with criminal records.

What Is the Darién Gap and Why Should We Shut It Down Permanently?

The Darién Gap is a sparsely populated, one hundred-mile-long by thirty-mile-wide jungle and swamp lands that connect Panama in Central America to Columbia in South America. It is also the starting location for millions of illegal alien caravans from Africa, South America, and most recently China. The area is home to about five indigenous tribes that total about eight thousand inhabitants.

The Darién Gap is one of the most dangerous places on earth, yet according to the New Humanitarian over 520,000 people still risked their lives and traversed the dangerous jungles and swamps through the jungles of Panama, through Costa Rica, into Nicaragua, then across Honduras, up through Guatemala, into Mexico, and from Mexico into the United States.[8]

Thankfully, due to the landscape and the terrain, there are no roads or even primitive paths to drive through, making the only way to travel through the Darién Gap by foot or possibly ferry. It is also one of the rainiest places on earth, resulting in dangerous mudslides and slippery footing conditions.

For those brave souls who risk traveling through the Darién Gap it is also completely unpoliced. There are wild animals and poisonous snakes to contend with, and let's not forget drug cartels, human traffickers, turf wars, drug smugglers, murderers, rapists, and thieves. The Darién Gap serves no purpose other than as another way for illegal aliens to travel to America. We need to shut it down permanently.

What if what is happening is not a border crisis at all but rather a purposeful border invasion?

Wouldn't aiding and abetting the invasion of the United States of America constitute as treason? United States Code 2381 states, "Whoever, owing allegiance to the United States, levies war against them, or adheres to their enemies, giving them aid and comfort within the United States or elsewhere, is guilty of treason."

Flying the Illegal Skies

The majority of illegal border crossers do so by foot, or by vehicle, but unbelievably a growing number of illegal aliens are being flown into America in the middle of the night by our own government! It's bad enough that the borders are wide open now. They are just breaking the law even further and flying these illegal aliens right in!

According to recent statistics from the U.S. Customs and Border Protection, the Biden administration, without the approval or knowledge of Congress, has made the unilateral decision to help America's continued invasion happen quicker by flying 404,000 illegal aliens into the United States.

This is "aiding and abetting an invasion" which is treason! The terrifying part is many of these immigrants are coming from Socialist or Communist countries like Cuba (84,000), Nicaragua (69,000), and Venezuela (95,000), or countries with unstable governments such as Haiti (154,000).

What's even more outrageous is that the Biden administration is flying these migrants into the United States of America's interior, oftentimes without the knowledge or consent of state officials and dropping them off in undisclosed locations. They admit to doing this, however, refuse to name all the different airports that are cooperating and keeping quiet about these secret flights.

So, I decided to do what I do best, and dug for the truth, and lo and behold, I found it!

Forty-Three Airports That Are Secretly Flying Illegal Aliens into America

These are the top fifteen airports based on number of people and frequency of flights from January 1, 2023, to August 30, 2023:

1. Miami, **Florida**—91,821
2. Fort Lauderdale, **Florida**—60,461
3. New York City, New York—14,827
4. Houston, Texas—7,923
5. Orlando, **Florida**—6,043
6. Los Angeles, California—3,271
7. Tampa, **Florida**—3,237

8. Dallas, Texas—2,256
9. San Francisco, California—2,052
10. Atlanta, Georgia—1,796
11. Newark, New Jersey—1,498
12. Washington, DC—1,472
13. Chicago, Illinois—496
14. Las Vegas, Nevada—483
15. Austin, Texas—171

If you total up all these numbers, you get 197,807. That is almost two hundred thousand people flown into our country from God knows where, unvetted, and dropped off at bus stops, train stations, airports, shelters, etc.

I also noticed something else. If you total up just the drop offs in the state of Florida, you get 161,562. So, this means at the top fifteen airports where the majority of these illegal immigrants were flown into, 81 percent are arriving in Florida, a state that is no longer a legitimate swing state and has been won handedly by the Republicans, but I am sure that is just another coincidence.

The remaining airports were named but either they are hiding the information on how many passengers are aboard the flights or the frequency of the arrivals was a much smaller number. Two trains of thought for which we do not have an answer at this time.

The other airports are: Albuquerque, New Mexico; Atlanta, Georgia; Baltimore, Maryland; Boston, Massachusetts; Cincinnati, Ohio; Columbus, Ohio; Charlotte, North Carolina; Denver, Colorado; Detroit, Michigan; Fresno, California; Honolulu, Hawaii; Indianapolis, Indiana; Kansas City, Missouri; Minneapolis, Minnesota; New Orleans, Louisiana; Philadelphia, Pennsylvania; Pittsburgh, Pennsylvania; Phoenix, Arizona; Portland, Oregon; Providence, Rhode Island; Raleigh-Durham, North Carolina; Sacramento, California; San Francisco, California; San Antonio, Texas; San Diego California; Seattle, Washington; Salt Lake City, Utah; and Tucson, Arizona.[9]

Can you take an educated guess as to who might be paying for all this? That's right, YOU the taxpayer! American taxpayers are secretly and unknowingly paying for their own invasion! If that doesn't turn those who are reading this into dedicated and focused activists, nothing will.

The Biden administration's CHNV parole program, which stands for Cuba, Haiti, Nicaragua, and Venezuela, allows illegals from these countries to apply for "humanitarian parole" in the United States where they can apply for work visas and gain employment for up to two years.

The cost of the airfare is almost always paid for by the government which means we-the-taxpayers. Moreover, because these illegals are being flown directly into the country, they are not counted in the official border statistics.[10]

Remember, the Biden administration's actions meet the threshold of US Code 18 2381 which states, "whoever owing allegiance to the United States, levies war against them, or adheres to their enemies, giving them aid and comfort within the United States or elsewhere is guilty of treason." The definition also talks about destroying the sovereignty of one's own nation—which has been allowed to happen to our country. It is treasonous.

What about the Northern Border of the United States?

Most of the focus and attention on illegal alien encounters are directed towards America's southern border. However, what about America's northern border? Are people sneaking into America through the Canadian provinces as well?

According to an April 2024 report from the Federation for American Immigration Reform, (FAIR) our northern border is seeing plenty of its own encounters with illegal aliens too. In fact, FAIR has reported a 114 percent increase of illegal alien encounters in the first quarter (four months) of 2024 alone.

In addition to the FAIR report, in May 2024, a report by the *New York Post* revealed border encounters at the northern border are expected to break the all-time record by the end of this year. Border Patrol agents recorded 9,460 migrant encounters at the United States-Canadian border between October 2023 and April 2024.

These numbers are at a record pace and there are still five more months to go. To give you an idea of how much of an increase this is, consider this comparison. In all of fiscal year 2023, Border Patrol agents recorded 10,021 illegal encounters and crossings at the northern border. This was a new record in 2023, and with five months still to go, the number of illegal encounters will likely smash last year's record.[11]

According to the study, the Swanton, Vermont sector is by far the busiest sector on the United States northern border. It covers Vermont and New Hampshire, plus five counties in New York State, all of which are also on the Canadian border with the province of Quebec. In fiscal year 2023, Swanton sector Border Patrol agents apprehended over 7,000 illegal aliens. To put this into perspective, that is more apprehensions than the last twelve years combined.

When one looks at the data in its entirety from the other northern border sectors it shows a troubling pattern. Every single sector has seen record-breaking encounters. In just the first four months of 2024, Border Patrol apprehended 4,772 people between the other ports of entry. That is a 114 percent increase over the first four months of 2023.[12]

The northern border is vastly different from the Southern border. Unlike the Southern border, the north does not have any man-made physical barriers, making it very easy to just walk across. Now, due to the Biden administration's catch-and-release policies, migrants have gotten smart and understand it is much easier and safer to sneak into America through the northern border than it is the southern border.

Migrants know it is better to take a flight into Canada and then safely walk across the border and into America than risk their lives traversing the terrains of the Darién Gap, the jungles of Panama, the mountains of Mexico, and the hot deserts of the Southwest. Not to mention the fact that they could be robbed, raped, or killed by the cartels or the traffickers.

How Do We Fix Our Borders Once and for All?

Here are three common sense solutions to secure our borders:

1. Every state is a border state because open borders affect the entire country. This means that every state should send their National Guard down to the southern border states to help stop the invasion. While the flow of illegal immigration is being halted, we must demand that our government permanently secures our borders by first finishing the southern border wall and then starting construction on a northern border wall as well.

2. Amnesty is never the right option. All it does is invite more illegal immigration. It is also very unfair to those who came to our country through the proper channels. So rounding up and deporting en masse every illegal alien with a criminal record should be a top priority. In addition, we must increase the penalties from a misdemeanor to a felony for being in the country illegally and reinstate and enforce the Remain in Mexico policy.

3. Next, we must remove the enticements to come here in the first place. We must eliminate the visa lottery as immigration should only be merit based. We must eliminate chain migration which will deter people from coming here illegally because they will not have their family and loved ones with them. Finally, we must eliminate birthright citizenship for illegal aliens. Just because you had a baby here doesn't mean you, and your family, should obtain automatic citizenship.

It is often said that a country that refuses to control and secure its own borders will eventually no longer be a country. Instead, it will be a weakened, more dangerous and often lawless place. The rate of illegal alien infiltration in the United States of America that we are being subjected to on a daily basis is not only reprehensible, but it is unsustainable and a dangerous national security risk.

Fixing our borders is the easy part, but finding politicians with the political will to do so is something entirely different. The Democratic Party doesn't believe in borders or even US sovereignty. They want to replace the white working-class voters they have abandoned. What better way of accomplishing this than to open and flood the borders.

Republicans are no better. They want to employ cheap labor and therefore would rather pay illegal aliens than American workers. The two-party duopoly wants to flood the country for different reasons and none of them are any good.

Closing our borders is not inhumane, it is not anti-immigrant, and it is not xenophobic either. What is inhumane is leaving them wide open. America is a loving and accepting country, but our generosity must have its limits and not be taken advantage of.

CHAPTER FOUR

Dismantling Washington, DC

This might be the most controversial chapter yet. If you are a Washington, DC insider, entrenched in the administrative state in a position from which it is very difficult to get fired, you're not going to like this chapter or my solutions. My number one goal in writing this book is to show, with cold hard facts, exactly how we are losing our liberties and what groups or organizations are responsible for it.

My secondary goal is to focus all my solutions on decentralizing the power structure of the administrative state, their grip on power, and ultimately the elimination of their entrenched statuses. One way of doing this is to provide bold and brave solutions that ultimately will remove their grip on power in Washington, DC and transfer it back to its rightful owners, "We the People."

Finally, I aim to educate and teach every American that they possess the power and control over Washington, DC and show them how to use it effectively. Draining the swamp from entrenched corrupt politicians from both parties is unfortunately these days not enough.

We can't just drain the swamp, because if we do, the politicians will just refill it with even more unsavory creatures than inhabited it before. The solution is not to just drain the swamp but fill it in with concrete and destroy it permanently. The reality is Washington, DC is not just broken; it is irreparable in its current form.

You're Fired!

Love him or hate him, one thing former President Trump was good at and was never afraid to do was fire people. Let's face it, we were watching *The Apprentice* to see who he was going to fire next, not hire.

However, in Washington, DC, firing people is a lot more complicated. Unfortunately, there are some folks in DC who have served several different administrations, both Republican and Democrat, and they can't be fired so easily.

Don't you think a new president, whether a Democrat or a Republican, deserves the right to take office with his or her own people? Why should a newly elected president get stuck with career bureaucrats who will try to undermine his or her agenda? A new president has enough to worry about and does not need bitter, angry, insubordinate partisan relics hanging around doing everything they can to obstruct the president's agenda.

Remember, it is true that political appointees by the president set the policies of the new administration; however, it is the career civil servants and the permanent administrative state that are responsible for its implementation.

Although by law, the administrative state is supposed to be non-partisan, it is anything but. Just ask President Trump if he thinks he was undermined by the administrative state. Hope you packed lunch because you're going to be there for a while. The administrative state tried to frame President Trump even before he took office? I wonder who told them to do that.

We all remember the "Russia, Russia, Russia" stories, right? Or how many countless times information was leaked to the *New York Times*? It was as if someone had Maggie Haberman on the speed dial.

A Few More Leaks to Jog Your Memory

1. The Steele Dossier: British MI6 officer Christopher Steele's unsubstantiated and salacious claims about President Trump and Russian prostitutes
2. Incoming National Security adviser Mike Flynn's private conversation with Russian ambassador Sergei Kislak
3. Recently fired and bitter FBI director James Comey admitted to leaking his personal memos to a friend who then promptly leaked them to the *New York Times*.

4. President Trump's phone call with Ukrainian president Volodymyr Zelenskyy

5. President Trump's phone call with Australian prime minister Malcolm Turnbull[1]

That was just five off the top of my head! President Trump's administration was leaking like a sieve! Every single day, for four years, no matter what he did, no matter what he said, he was constantly being undermined and obstructed by the entrenched administrative state.

However, it is not just President Trump who has suffered these constant and damaging leaks. Democratic President Barack Obama saw his fair share of leaks as well. His administration, however, did a lot of the leaking on purpose.

When they needed the media to help them with a policy or legislation, they strategically leaked it. When it was something that painted the Obama administration in a negative light or exposed something they were trying to hide, Obama's Department of Justice was quick to prosecute.

A Few Major Leaks from the Obama Administration You Might Remember

1. Former CIA contractor Edward Snowden's leak of the PRISM program exposed Obama's National Security Agency's secret surveillance program.

2. The *New York Times* leak of Barack Obama's "Kill Lists"

3. The *Washington Post*'s leak on how the United States and Israel were behind the "Stuxnet" cyber-attack against Iran

4. Obama's Justice Department secretly obtained the Associated Press's emails and tracked visits by journalist James Rosen to the State Department.[2]

In 1978, Congress passed and Jimmy Carter signed into law the Civil Service Reform Act. This act overhauled the Federal Personnel and Payroll System by supposedly hiring people on merit and not political favors.

It also made it much harder to fire administrative state personnel by creating the Merit Systems Protection Board (MSPB) which established stronger protections for all federal employees against arbitrary actions such as wrongful terminations by appointing a review board to oversee such actions.

Once these entrenched career administrative state personnel realized they had these new protections, many of them became insubordinate or worse and just decided to work against whichever administration's policies they disagreed with. So much for the merit system.

It is for these reasons laid out above that we need to permanently rein in the administrative state. There is no logical reason why an incoming administration should be subjected to the remaining personnel, especially from the opposing party's administration. That is why I propose this to stop the madness.

Ending the Administrative State Act

If we are going to get serious about permanently draining the swamp, we will also need to permanently fill it in too. I propose that as soon as the next president-elect wins the general election, every member of the previous administration is put on notice.

Under the proposed Ending the Administrative State Act, once the transition team is established, every former official must reapply for their jobs within thirty days. If they fail to reapply within that time frame, they will be automatically terminated. If they decide to reapply for their jobs or another job inside the new administration, the transition team would have sixty days to decide whether or not to retain them or terminate them.

This would give the new administration the autonomy and control to decide not just who will be in their Cabinet, but also who will not be part of their administration. It will keep the new president from being undermined as well as drastically cut down on leaks. This will also allow the new president to truly call it their own administration.

"But Wait, You Can't Fire Us!"

Actually, yes, we can, and we must. Now, I know I am risking future invitations to Washington, DC cocktail parties; however, I think I can manage the heartbreak. As I mentioned previously, the government should be as small and as inconsequential to all of our lives as humanly possible.

Along with forcing individuals who make up the administrative state to reapply for their jobs, we need to change their classification to a schedule F status. In 2020, President Trump issued Executive Order 13957, which created a new classification for Federal Civil Service Employees who were working in positions that were privy to sensitive information.

This executive order made it easier to terminate administrative state personnel who worked in sensitive positions that dealt with classified documents or information, confidentiality agreements, policy making decisions, or foreign policy.

Sadly, President Trump's executive order was rescinded by Joe Biden. However, just as easily as one executive order can be rescinded, another can be reapplied. Instead of going back and forth every four years, voters who want to permanently drain the swamp need to pressure their elected officials to create and introduce this proposal. If congress passed legislation that mirrors my suggestions, reining in the administrative state would be yet another way to create more permanent freedom and preserve our liberties.

Most of Washington, DC vehemently opposes reclassification of federal workers to a schedule F, however, that is exactly why I like this idea so much. Hopefully, a brave anti-establishment member of Congress will learn about EASA and have the intestinal fortitude to introduce it in the next Congress.

Speaking of Congress, Let's Talk About How to Curtail Their Power

Congress was never designed to be a full-time career. Our Founding Fathers feared what today's politicians have turned into; lying, thieving, corrupt, power-hungry, full-time politicians. It is clear to just about any American across the political spectrum that most of our members of Congress are more interested in serving their own personal needs rather than the needs of their constituents.

Originally, being a member of Congress was indeed seen as a part-time role. In fact, many of America's earliest lawmakers had other primary careers such as farmers, lawyers, teachers, and businessmen. Many early lawmakers were reluctant to serve in Congress. Others did it purely as another way to serve their country, and not themselves.

Notably, most of those who served in Congress at that time in our history did so by living outside of the Washington, DC area as well. The majority of America's earliest lawmakers actually still had businesses to run and jobs to attend as well as families to help raise and support. In the earlier years of our republic, congressional sessions were also much shorter in duration than they are now; typically, only lasting a few months.

Washington, DC is roughly sixty-eight square miles, yet there are over twelve thousand five hundred registered lobbyists. That is approximately 183 lobbyists per square mile!

That is a lot of centralized power, influence peddling, kickbacks, and corruption. This is why Congress needs to go back to being a part-time job and all 535 members need to work from their respective states rather than from inside the confines of Washington, DC.[3]

According to the 118th Congress, which convened on January 3, 2023 and will conclude to January 3, 2025, the US Senate will only be in session for 154 days, and the US House of Representatives will be in session for only 117 days.

So, switching these members of Congress to a part-time work schedule will not be a shock to any of their systems, as they barely work as it is. Considering a full-time American worker spends on average roughly 260 days per year working full time at their jobs, our members of Congress are already working part-time hours, and for particularly good compensation too.

The average US Senator and House of Representatives salary is $174,000 per year. Not too bad for only working between 115 and 160 days a year. How many Americans would jump at the opportunity to be paid that much while only having to work a part-time schedule?[4]

However, in today's political climate it seems now more than ever that serving in Congress is in many ways a legal license to steal. One could argue that today's politicians no longer serve the will of their constituents; unless of course, those constituents have loads of cash to buy many of them off.

In the year 2024, with all our advanced technology, do we really need 535 politicians, surrounded by thousands of lobbyists, activists, and contractors centrally located in only sixty-eight square miles of influence, corruption, power, and greed? Of course not. But how do you remove the political class from their cozy little swamp?

Poet and playwright Oscar Wilde once famously said, "life imitates art far more than art imitates life." In today's high-tech and advanced society, television cartoons we watched as children, such as *The Jetsons*, first introduced us to many gadgets we now use today.

According to a review by *PC Magazine*, the Jetsons were using futuristic technology and showing us what our future might look like. The incredible part is they were showing us these gadgets in the 1960s.

Five Gadgets We Saw on *The Jetsons* Cartoon That We Use Today

1. Video calls—George, Elroy, and Mr. Spacely, you may remember, all had video screens they used to communicate with one another.
2. Personal robot assistants—Do you remember "Rosy the Robot"? We have companies like Boston Dynamics, Google, and Amazon that have fully functioning robots. We also have Alexa, Siri, Echo, and other voice-operated devices.
3. Smartwatches—Many phones are now wearable as watches. Apple, Google, and Samsung now all make smartwatches.
4. Food printing—Many episodes showed the Jetson family members turning on their food replicator and printing out a meal. In 2006, Cornell University developed a 3D food printer to use for chocolate and cookie dough.
5. Space travel—How could we ever forget watching the Jetsons traveling through space in their flying cars? Flying cars could be the next gadget that comes to fruition in the future as well.[5]

Super advanced computers, artificial intelligence, digital currency, possibly flying cars, and the rise of machines; it seems as though technology is advancing at speeds that are hard to believe or comprehend. *The Jetsons* gave us a small but powerful glimpse into the future and are a shining example of how life can imitate art.

How many science fiction movies or television shows have you watched in your lifetime and said to yourself, "Oh, that will never happen, it's just a movie." Well, lights, camera, and action! Our lives are now reminiscent of many old movies and television shows, except now we are the stars.

We live in a world so technologically advanced that at times nothing seems too impossible. The constant advancements in almost every sector of our society have affected our lives by creating a more mobile society. We live in a time where you can start your car, turn on and off your lights in your house, and even check your blood pressure, all by using your smartphone.

There is simply no reason why our members of Congress cannot conduct their official business for the people from their respective state capitals. Think about how much money they would save in housing and travel expenses alone? As Bob Dylan's famous 1964 song goes, "The Times They Are A-Changin.'"

According to a recent survey from *Forbes*, by next year in 2025, an estimated 32.6 million Americans will be working remotely instead of in an office. Many of these workers only need to show up in person for special events such as important meetings, training seminars, or in some cases minimum in-person requirements. This means that roughly 22 percent of the entire workforce in America could eventually be working remotely.[6]

With business-friendly tools such as Zoom, Google Meet, and Skype, as well as social media, text messaging, and of course email correspondence, there are no shortages of technology that could be used to perform the everyday functions of Congress from OUTSIDE of Washington, DC.

By sending our representatives back to their respective states to conduct official business, we would immediately decentralize the influence and power structure in Washington, DC. This would make it more difficult for power brokers, activist groups, and lobbyists to influence national politics and fiscal policy.

Term Limits: About the Only Thing Most Americans Agree On

It is often said politicians are like dirty diapers, they need to be changed and changed often. After we send our representatives back home to their respective states, let's also limit their time in which they can "serve" us. The support for term limits on our elected officials by the American people has strong bipartisan support. The data shows the American public are fed up with entrenched career politicians.

However, with all the money, kickbacks, corruption, lavish gifts, exotic trips, and payoffs, very few politicians are willing to voluntarily vote to limit their time in office. Most polls show that an overwhelming majority of Americans, regardless of political party or persuasion, believe in term limits for our elected officials.

According to a Gallup poll from January 2023, three out of four voters, (75 percent) want Congress to enact term limits. Only 21 percent of respondents said they were not in favor of cutting the time a member of Congress could serve.

Republicans support term limits 82 percent to 15 percent. Independents favor term limits 79 percent to 17 percent, and Democrats support term limits 65 percent to 29 percent.[7]

Wow! Something most of the American people can agree on! This one topic politically is a winning issue for both parties. The only people who are really against it are our politicians.

This is why I propose two six-year terms for the US Senate and four two-year terms for the US House of Representatives.

In addition, we must fight to keep our last line of defense from becoming our biggest obstacle to preserving freedom. Many political pundits and constitutional scholars, who agree with term limits for our elected officials, do not agree with term limits for our Supreme Court justices.

They argue that the Supreme Court would lack judicial stability. They argue that it could be counterproductive to remove good judges. These are all legitimate arguments; however, I disagree wholeheartedly, and here is the reason why.

Sometimes when a new justice is nominated and confirmed to the Supreme Court, it may take a few years or a couple of important decisions to find out if that justice will be an originalist judge and interpret the constitution as it is written, or instead look for ways to circumvent it. It is for this reason that it is imperative not to allow lifetime appointments on our highest court.

This is why I propose a ten-year term for all Supreme Court justices, which should be standard with an opportunity at reconfirmation for another ten-year term. This should keep activist judges from serving a lifetime and originalist judges from becoming corrupt over time.

Time to Rein In Our Shadow Court

What if I told you there was another court in America that works almost entirely in secrecy and is accountable to no one. What if I also told you that this court is almost as powerful and influential as our Supreme Court, however, none of its judges are confirmed through a Senate confirmation.

And finally, what if I also told you the decisions they make are not typically discussed publicly, they approve over 99 percent of their cases, and all eleven judges are appointed by the chief justice of the Supreme Court.

You might think I'm crazy or reciting some line from a science fiction movie; however, the truth is this court does exist, it is legal, and it is known as the United States Foreign Intelligence Surveillance Court, more commonly known as the FISA Court.

The FISA Court was established on October 25, 1978. For forty-six years, this court has been rubber stamping our rights away by approving oftentimes unnecessary and unconstitutional warrants on American citizens.

Since its inception, the FISA Court has issued 33,942 warrants, denying only twelve of them! For anyone who's paying close attention, that is a rejection rate of only 0.03 percent. This means, this secretive court, without oversight, and whose judges do not have to be confirmed, is approving 99.96 percent of every single warrant that is put in front of them![8]

We Need to Rein In the FISA Court

It is unconscionable to think that for the last forty-six years, we have allowed a shadow court to approve over 99 percent of warrants placed in front of them without public knowledge or scrutiny and with absolutely zero oversight. This must change immediately.

This is why I am proposing that every FISA judge must be confirmed through the advice and consent nomination process of the US Senate. All Supreme Court justices have to be confirmed to the highest court, so why wouldn't every FISA judge be subjected to the same approval process?

Moreover, the chief justice of the US Supreme Court, in this case John G. Roberts Jr., should NOT be in charge of confirming the FISA Court judges. Finally, these judges and their decisions on approving or denying warrants should be public record and not decided in secrecy. Reining in the

FISA Court is yet another way to weaken the administrative state, and of course, preserve more of our liberties.

Platform Voting Keeps Politicians' Promises

So many of our politicians get elected by promising the voters that when they are elected, they will keep all their campaign promises. The problem is the vast majority never do. I believe in actions, not words—and accountability. Something elected officials try to circumnavigate.

One way to hold elected officials to their campaign promises is to tie their reelection chances to their votes. Every election cycle, both parties update their party's platform through steering committees. This is where they decide what their legislative goals will be for the upcoming term. What if we had a way to hold our elected officials accountable by their votes?

I know what you are thinking, we already do through the voting process. That may be true; however, wouldn't it be better if they were graded on how close their votes lined up with their party's official platform instead? The truth is they already are, but this powerful tool is not being used properly.

Libertyscore.conservativereview.com is a website that grades every elected member by the type of votes they cast. Politicians are graded from an F to an A just like in grade school. What if we had an 80 percent threshold that every elected official had to be above based on their party's official platform?

If a politician falls below the threshold at the end of their first year in office, they are given a warning. If after the end of their second year in office they are still below the minimum threshold, they would be forced to resign their seat and let someone else run instead.

I get it, these are liberty-based and focused radical ideas. But what is more radical, letting these entrenched career criminals continue to serve indefinitely? Sometimes this is the type of thinking that we need to have if we are ever going to hold our elected officials accountable for the promises, they make to us. Moreover, this would also work as a "de facto" term limits due to the ability to remove elected officials who do not keep their promises.

The truth is absolute power corrupts absolutely. If we remove the magnets to that corruption we can decentralize power, shrink the size of the federal government, and return more power back to the people.

CHAPTER FIVE

Houston, We Have a Spending Problem

One of the greatest threats America faces, (*besides agitating Russia, another nuclear power, and goading them into World War Three*) is our enormous national debt and irresponsible and deliberate fiscal policy.

Continuous deficit spending, with no end in sight, and no political will-power or appetite in Washington, DC to curb their thirst for our tax dollars, is what has gotten us to this place. If we do not pass a balanced budget amendment, this unsustainable gravy train of ludicrous spending will bring our country's inflation to levels that would rival Robert Mugabe's Zimbabwe.

Our elected officials know we are in a fiscal crisis that they created, yet they just don't seem to care. They are so blinded by their own self-importance and indulgence to even think about anyone else but themselves.

Have you ever heard of a piece of legislation that was signed into law in 1917 called the Second Liberty Bond Act? In modern times and in today's political context it is now known as "The Debt Ceiling." The Second Liberty Bond Act was introduced and signed into law during World War One in order to help finance America's participation in the war.

The law allowed the United States Treasury to issue wartime bonds without congressional approval until the debt reached a predetermined monetary ceiling. Think of the original debt ceiling as a wartime credit card with a limit.

However, after reaching the limit, instead of paying off the country's debt or at least trying to pay it down, the government decided instead to just print more money. This was the equivalent of essentially raising the limit on their own credit cards and proceeding to spend even more money they know they have no intention to ever pay back.

The debt ceiling is the aggregate amount of financial liabilities the United States federal government is authorized to pay in order to meet its existing obligations. This consists of Social Security and Medicare benefits, military and federal employee salaries, and of course, the interest payments on the national debt.

The precise number of times the debt ceiling has been raised, according to information on the United States Department of the Treasury's own website, is an incredible seventy-eight times since its inception in 1917! What started out as a way to finance World War One and eventually World War Two, has now metastasized into a fiscally irresponsible and dangerous game of "kick the can down the road."[1]

In the twenty-first century, the debt ceiling debates have turned into a three-ring circus with both political parties using the debt ceiling as a threat against the other. For example, in 2011 and 2013, the debt ceiling debate brought the United States to the brink of default. In fact, for the first time in United States history, our government received its first credit rating downgrade.

Take Away Washington, DC's Credit Card

The federal government has had at least seventy-eight separate opportunities to address the debt ceiling and every time they voted to raise it, instead of facing the problem head on. There are too many fat and bloated piggies at the trough munching away on taxpayer's dollars to be even the slightest bit concerned about the fiscal health and wellbeing of the country.

Every few years, when Congress starts to reach their artificially self-imposed debt ceiling limit, it becomes an immediate focus and their number one priority. Once Washington, DC realizes their supply is running low, they act like drug addicts on a three-day binge and look to the taxpayers to supply them with their next fix.

This is when they summon their lackeys in the media to start talking about how we are approaching a crisis (*that they created*), and to avoid the fiscal cliff, we must raise the debt ceiling immediately.

Next comes the fear mongering and the lie about how if we don't raise the debt ceiling, the federal government will shut down and all the poor federal workers will starve to death. Well, you are certainly not going to receive any sympathy from this writer. I say shut it down and keep it closed.

The Government Shutdown Lie

Let's also address this notion that somehow when there is a "government shutdown" the federal government actually shuts down. Newsflash—it does not shutdown. This is just the political class trying to put pressure and guilt on unsuspecting taxpayers, who don't know that during a "government shutdown," the government doesn't really shut down.

During a so-called "government shutdown," some operations of the federal government, which are considered non-essential, are halted temporarily. However, most of the government is still open and functioning.

Nonessential parts of the federal government may remain closed such as museums and national parks, but even these workers are reimbursed their back pay once the shutdown is over. Secretly, these workers are probably thrilled they get the extra time off knowing that they will still get paid for it.

Services that are considered essential are not interrupted during a so-called government shutdown. These services include but are not limited to defense and national security, military operations, public safety services, law enforcement personnel, prison operations, and air traffic controllers. All these essential functions of the government stay open, as well as medical centers, firehouses, public utility companies, and power grid operations.

As mentioned previously, in regard to back pay and furloughs, many of these federal workers, or as I like to call them, nonessential employees, will still be reimbursed once the federal government reopens. So, during so-called government shutdowns the government never really does shut down.

One reason why politicians from both parties refuse to address the debt ceiling is it can be used as a political weapon against the party in power. Politicians use the debt ceiling debate to score political points and find new ways to waste more of the taxpayer's money, while refusing to address the problem head on that they created.

Another Great Way to Drain the Swamp—Shut It Down

The very least amount of time our federal government is open, the better off we all are. Another way to "drain the swamp" is to finally do the right thing and shut down the government the next time we reach the next debt ceiling debate.

We have established the fact that during a government shutdown the federal government still functions and operates, and we also know that those workers will still be reimbursed and given their back pay as soon as the shutdown is over. If that's the case, how about we really shut down the federal government, and for a good long time too.

If we actually did shut down the government, with the only exception being that of our military and safety services, think of how many administrative state personnel would eventually be forced to find another job?

Let's say for argument's sake, we did shut down the federal government for at least sixty days. We would then have a chance to eliminate probably half of the administrative state, including the eight thousand plus Senior Executive Services personnel, (SES), or as I like to call them, nonessential workers. The longer Washington, DC stays closed, the more freedom Americans can enjoy and the less federal workers we would have.

Most, if not all spending in Washington, DC is without merit. Government spending on what are known as pet projects or pork barrel spending is completely out of control. Hundreds of thousands of these ridiculous and unconscionable discretionary spending projects are one reason why our country is over thirty-four trillion dollars in debt.

According to a recent report from CNBC, our national debt increases one trillion dollars about every one hundred days. Who knows, maybe by the time this book goes to print our national debt will have eclipsed thirty-five trillion?[2]

Our discretionary spending spree doesn't seem to be slowing down anytime soon either. In fact, it seems as though the problem is getting worse. According to the watchdog organization Citizens Against Government Waste (CAGW), even drunken sailors would be jealous of our members of Congress. CAGW tracks all spending in Washington, DC and has been fighting for fiscal responsibility and, quite frankly, sanity since 1984.

In 2023, CAGW's annual congressional pig book identified 7,396 different pet projects totaling a cost of $26.1 billion dollars. This was an increase of 43.9 percent more than the 5,138 pet projects identified in fiscal year 2022.

Moreover, the $26.1 billion in fiscal year 2023 was the third highest amount since 1991. In fact, since 1991 CAGW has identified 124,212 total pet projects costing taxpayers $437.5 billion dollars![3]

To give you an idea of how much money that is in wasteful spending, consider that the total economies of Venezuela ($211.9 billion), Honduras ($75.7 billion), Nicaragua ($54.8 billion), Guyana ($55.5 billion), and Madagascar ($37.5 billion) are about equal to what our Congress wasted on discretionary spending!

A Partial List of Some of the Most Insane and Outrageous Pet Projects

1. *The famous bridge to Nowhere*—This one is number one for a reason. This notorious 2005 pet project authorized $452 million dollars to build two bridges in Alaska, one of which would have connected the city of Ketchikan (population 7,966) to Gravina Island (population 49 people) The bridge, which was thankfully never built, would have cost $398 million dollars to build for less than 50 people?

2. *The Turtle Tunnel*—As part of the unnecessary $787 billion-dollar porkulus bill, $3.4 million of it was set aside for a turtle crossing underneath Highway 27 in Tallahassee, Florida. Sadly for taxpayers, the turtle tunnel project was completed in 2010. But why stop there, in 2023 Dakota County, Minnesota built another turtle crossing. I guess we know now how the turtles crossed the road.[4]

3. *Shrimp on a treadmill*—Yes folks, seriously. In 2007, The National Science Foundation, which is bankrolled by our federal government, earmarked $500,000 to study the mobility of shrimp by making the little critters run on tiny treadmills. After three years of study and $3 million dollars later, what did this study teach us? I don't know about

you but when I go out to a nice seafood restaurant, I always ask the waitress if the shrimp have had a good workout before I eat them.

4. ***Robo Squirrel***—Researchers at San Diego State University received a grant from the National Science Foundation for $325,000 dollars to create a robotic squirrel that gets attacked by a rattlesnake. Researchers wanted to study how the heat signatures of a squirrel's tail confused the rattlesnakes. My first question would be, "How can there be a heat signature in a robotic squirrel?"[5]

5. ***The Teapot Museum***—In 2005, Congress set aside $500,000 to build the Sparta Teapot Craft and Museum in Sparta, North Carolina, which has a population of about eighteen thousand people. Apparently, there wasn't a real desire to look at different colored and shaped teapots as the museum closed in January of 2010.[6]

If you thought those five earmarks were bad, here is Senator Rand Paul's annual report on wasteful spending. This was from 2020, and it is still shocking. According to his report, 5.4 million Americans spent $54 billion dollars on stuff like this:

1. ***$1.3 million*** to study whether Americans will eat ground-up bugs. Let me save you the suspense, the answer is no. I wonder if the World Economic Forum and Klaus Schwab were behind this study?

2. ***$2 million*** to study whether hot tubbing can help lower stress. How would this study even work? Do we have to buy $2 million worth of hot tubs? How many people per tub? At what temperature does the hot tub relieve stress? This one is impressive.

3. ***$1.5 million*** to study lizards now on the treadmill! Well, it worked so well for the shrimp, right? Honestly, I think lizards would probably do a better job than shrimp. Perhaps we can spend another ten million more dollars building a racetrack to study who would win in a race, the shrimp or the lizard?

4. ***$1.4 million*** on a study to see if we can finally get those darn Eastern Mediterranean kids to stop smoking hookah! Apparently, the hookah problem is so bad with the Eastern Mediterranean kids, that we need American taxpayers to help find a solution.

5. And the Winner is . . . drum roll please . . . **$*4.5 million*** to study the effects of alcoholic rats when they are sprayed with bobcat urine! This one is so crazy the joke writes itself.[7]

On a more serious note, none of what you just read is funny, it is actually sad. It goes to show you that these politicians will spend our money, without our permission, on things we don't need or would ever want. This type of insane spending is bankrupting our country, and it needs to stop.

"Inflation is not caused by the actions of private citizens, but by the government: by an artificial expansion of the money supply required to support deficit spending. No private embezzlers or bank robbers in history have ever plundered people's savings on a scale comparable to the plundering perpetrated by the fiscal policies of statist governments." —Ayn Rand[8]

That is a true and powerful quote indeed. Here is one I just thought of to go along with it. "What you give to the government, the government will always take. So do not consent to that which is unconstitutional regarding fiscal policy. Remember, any individual, whether well versed or not in financial matters, can always manage their own finances better than the government can spend it." —Josh Bernstein

Tick Tock Debt Clock

As of April 2024, according to the constantly changing by-the-second website usdebtclock.org, our national debt is an astonishing $34.6 ***trillion***. If every American citizen decided to pay off the US debt, it would cost all 336 million Americans approximately $267,000 each!

This insane amount of debt our country owes is not only completely unsustainable, but also a major threat to our national security. The United States of America has carried debt since its inception. This was due to the fact that the Revolutionary War was financed by other nations.

Many of our Founding Fathers, led by Benjamin Franklin, secured loans for millions of dollars from other countries in order to finance their war efforts. Our Founding Fathers always knew debt would be inevitable.

I mean, who starts a country with no money right? Sure, they would have loved to start a new country on their charm alone, but it just wasn't in the cards. Instead, they did what they had to do, and nobody faults them for that.

However, we have had 248 years to take our financial insolvency seriously, and yet we have chosen not to. We are one of the world's greatest superpowers, yet we are also the world's biggest debtor nation.

Benjamin Franklin and the boys knew the country would have some debt; they just didn't think it would consist of thirteen zeros. When you add in the interest and unfunded liabilities on our national debt, the number would likely cause an error on most calculators.

Here's another dizzying figure, The US's national debt including unfunded liabilities and the interest on thirty-four trillion dollars is a staggering $215 *trillion*! We are not in debt; we are on life support.

To give you an idea how dangerous this is, as of February 2024, according to Reuters, the global debt was $313 *trillion*. If I did the math right, that would mean that the United States of America's unfunded liabilities on our national debt is 68 percent of the total global world debt!

Two Radical New Ways to Pay Down Our National Debt Using Thirteen Zeros

Now that we have established from the data on the United States Debt Clock that in order to pay off our national debt we would need $267,000 from each tax paying US citizen, what can we do to start chipping away at this seemingly insurmountable mountain of debt?

We can clearly see, based on demographics alone, that very few Americans have the financial capacity and access to that kind of money, however some do. So, then the question remains, how do we incentivize the wealthier Americans who do have that kind of money to pay it towards the national debt?

According to a 2024 snapshot by Millennial Money, the United States of America has 22 million millionaires and 735 billionaires. If all 22 million millionaires and 735 billionaires paid $267,000 dollars each in exchange for a lifetime exemption on paying future taxes, that amount of money paid towards the national debt would be $5,874,196,245,000, which has thirteen zeros.[9]

If given the option, how many of the wealthiest Americans would consider this proposal? I would venture to guess many of the US millionaires and billionaires would be thrilled to do so. America's wealthiest individuals and their personal wealth will likely continue to grow for many years to come.

We have all heard the saying, "the more you make the more they take" right? As these wealthy Americans continue to grow their vast fortunes, they will have to pay higher and higher percentages of their income to taxes. Who wouldn't want to pay a one-time fee for a lifetime of future exemptions?

Four Trillion More

According to taxpolicycenter.org, US taxpayers are hiding close to four trillion dollars in offshore accounts. The Foreign Account Tax Compliance Act (FATCA) requires foreign banks and investment management firms to report information about accounts owned and controlled by American taxpayers.

To corroborate the above data, using confidential administrative data reported under FATCA, financial analysts estimate about 1.5 million United States taxpayers are holding roughly four trillion dollars in offshore accounts in places with low to no taxes such as Switzerland, Luxembourg, or the Cayman Islands.[10]

The highest capital gains tax rate in the world is Denmark at 42 percent. The US's top short-term capital gains tax rate is 37 percent, which is not too far behind. It is clear the majority of these assets are being held outside of the United States for tax purposes. What if we gave these American taxpayers an incentive to bring this money back home?

How many of these 1.5 million American taxpayers wouldn't want the same deal to pay $267,000 in a one-time payment towards the National Debt? Let's assume all take the government up on the offer. That is another four hundred billion dollars towards the national debt. I know that barely even pays for the interest. True, but here's a way to get the four trillion back.

How about a lifetime zero percent capital gains tax rate if all their
assets are transferred back into America's economy, banks, investment
companies, and other financial institutions?

If this was to occur, the four trillion dollars would be a huge boost to our
economy and much of these assets would be recirculated throughout every
sector of our economy. This would secure another four trillion dollars
towards paying down the national debt.

Moreover, if we were able to pay nine trillion dollars towards our national
debt, that would drop our debt level down to what it was pre-Covid, which
was close to twenty-five trillion.[11]

I understand wiping out a little more than $9 trillion of our $34 trillion
national debt is like putting a Band-Aid on a gunshot wound, but we've got
to do something. This may not put the country back into solvency, but it is
a start in the right direction.

Remember, this is just the super wealthy. What about all the other
Americans who owe that amount or more in back taxes? This could be a new
and creative way to solve two problems at once; paying down our national
debt and getting Americans to no longer have to pay taxes. Sounds like a
win-win to me.

Now that we have established that our elected representatives are willing
to spend our money on things like shrimps and lizards on treadmills, turtle
crossings, and bridges to nowhere, it is safe to say we need to take away their
credit cards and do it quickly.

**That is why I am proposing that all discretionary spending be rele-
gated to the state governments. For instance, any pet project, study, or
earmark that a member of Congress wants to introduce must instead be
approved and voted on by the taxpayers of each respective state.**

The most effective and financially responsible way to give taxpayers back
control over spending is through petitions and ballot initiatives. This will
allow each state, and not their members of Congress, to decide what they
want or don't want to spend their taxpayer dollars on.

If the people of Montana want to spend money studying the hiberna-
tion habits of grizzly bears, they should have the opportunity to do so, or
not. If Floridians want to study the mating habits of manatees, they should
have the option as to whether or not they want to pay for it.

Surprisingly, Congress has shown a propensity to stop these pet projects in the past and did so for about ten years, so we know it can happen again. However, in 2021, both parties couldn't resist running up our debt more and wasting our money, so they brought them back with a vengeance. It is time we had a constitutional amendment banning these pet projects permanently.

CHAPTER SIX

An Armed Society Is a Polite Society

"A well-regulated militia, being necessary to the security of a free state, the right of the people to keep and bear arms shall not be infringed." These words are perhaps the most important words in American history. The Second Amendment, one could argue, is the most important of all amendments in the United States Constitution. Many have said that it should be the first amendment because it protects all other amendments.

The right to self-defense, enshrined in our Constitution, must be defended vigorously and at all costs. This right is a critical element of the American constitutional framework intended to empower individuals and ensure there remains a balance between the federal government and the freedoms and liberties of the people in which they govern.

This is why it is imperative that any attempts to limit the purchase or possession of firearms must always be defeated. The ability to thwart any attempts by an overreaching tyrannical government is the fundamental reason for the Second Amendment. As history often has demonstrated, millions upon millions of people became subjects and were exterminated by their governments once they were disarmed.

When the government fears the people there is freedom. When the people fear the government there is tyranny. An armed republic forces our government to use reason and restraint when negotiating with We the People.

If America was not the most armed country in the world, (120 firearms per 100 people)[1] our government would have no reason to negotiate with the people using anything else but force.

First Is Registration, Second Is Confiscation, Third Is Extermination

History has shown that an unarmed country does not stand a chance against a fully armed government. From Adolf Hitler to Joesph Stalin to Vladimir Lenin to Mao Ze Dong, all of these dictators had one thing in common. They all disarmed their people and systematically exterminated their political rivals and enemies.

Adolf Hitler, who was the leader of the Nazi Party, established the German Weapons Act of 1938. This act, which was primarily drafted by Heinrich Himmler, the head of Hitler's SS and Gestapo, was one of the major architects of the Holocaust.

This act gave the Nazi Party unrestricted and complete control over all German citizens' right to possess firearms. From 1938 until 1945, it is estimated that thirteen million people including six million Jews were exterminated as a direct result of the Nazi Party's gun control measures.

In 1942, Adolf Hitler said this in regard to gun control: "The most foolish mistake we could possibly make would be to allow the subject races the right to possess arms. History shows that all conquerors, who have allowed their subjects to carry arms, have prepared their own downfall by doing so."

Hitler continues, "Indeed, I would go so far as to say that the supply of arms to the underdogs is a sine qua non for the overthrow of any sovereignty. So, let's not have any native militia or native police. German troops alone will bear the sole responsibility for the maintenance of law and order throughout the occupied Russian territories, and a system of military strong points must be evolved in order to cover the entire occupied country." — Adolf Hitler (1941–1944)[2]

In case you were wondering, a sine qua non is a Latin term that means, "without which not." It translates to an essential element, development, or condition that must occur in order to facilitate a certain result. Hitler knew the only way he had a shot at world domination was to confiscate all firearms in the occupied territories. Thankfully, America and the Allied Forces thought otherwise and defeated Hitler in World War Two.

Or how about Joseph Stalin's gun control quote from 1929: "If the opposition disarms, all well and good. If it refuses to do so, we shall disarm it ourselves. "Although there are competing numbers in regard to how many people Joseph Stalin was responsible for killing, American historian William D. Rubenstein has concluded that, even under the most conservative estimates, Joseph Stalin was directly responsible for the deaths of at least seven million people. This number represents roughly 4.2 percent of the former USSR's population at that time.[3]

However, no one in world history has been responsible for as many deaths as the Chinese dictator Mao Zedong. Mao's reign of terror started in 1949 when the People's Republic of China was first established.

Chairman Mao's reign of terror lasted approximately twenty-seven years. It is estimated that as many as seventy million people died as a result of his policies, including as many as forty-five million in only four years due to Chairman Mao's Great Leap Forward Cultural Revolution.[4]

This program, which ran from 1958 until 1962, aimed to rapidly change China from an agrarian economy to one of a Socialist society through the use of rapid industrialization and collectivization. Finally, Mao's second and final revolution, known officially as the Great Proletarian Cultural Revolution, lasted ten years, from 1966 until his death in 1976.[5]

Estimates of the total death toll vary; however, with executions of political adversaries routine, widespread famine throughout the country, and forced labor camps, it is estimated that as many as eighty million people died as a direct result of Mao's policies.[6]

Here was Mao Zedong's take on gun control, "All political power comes from the barrel of a gun. The Communist Party must command all the guns, that way no guns could ever be used to command the Communist Party."

These lessons in history are a stark reminder of why America's Second Amendment is the most important amendment we have in our Constitution. Gun Control in any form is not only un-American, but more importantly it is the antithesis to everything we hold dear as Americans, most significantly the right to protect ourselves. Gun control measures go against the very nature of what freedom represents.

From Our Cold Dead Hands

Even with all the above-mentioned examples throughout world history of what happens when a country's leaders confiscate firearms from their citizens, American politicians either haven't learned from history or are just plain ignoring it. It is for this reason that any politician who has ever introduced any type of gun control legislation is unfit to lead and represent the people of this country.

In the twentieth century, significant federal legislation began to shape modern gun control. In 1934, Congress passed the unconstitutional National Firearms Act of 1934. This was the first significant law to regulate the manufacturing, distribution, and possession of certain firearms. The NFA was part of Franklin Delano Roosevelt's "New Deal" which was the largest expansion of government overreach in American history at that time.

The National Firearms Act targeted specific types of firearms such as machine guns, short barrel or sawed-off shotguns, concealable handguns, and suppressors (commonly known today as silencers).[7]

The next significant piece of unconstitutional legislation was the 1938 Federal Firearms Act.

Isn't it interesting that while the Nazi Party in Germany was disarming its citizens in 1938, so too was the American government trying to disarm the American people, and in the same year.

This act, another intrusive parallel to the 1934 Act, was designed to curb crime by regulating the interstate commerce of firearms. The act required all manufacturers, importers, and dealers of firearms to obtain a federal firearms license from the Secretary of Commerce.[8]

The last major piece of unconstitutional legislation that was passed in the last century was the Firearms Control Regulations Act of 1975. This Act unconstitutionally imposed very stringent restrictions on the ownership, registration, and storage of firearms within the District of Columbia.

This unconstitutional gun control act mandated that all firearms in private possession had to be registered (*there's that first step word again*) with the Metropolitan Police Department. Furthermore, it prohibited residents of Washington, DC from owning a firearm at their private residence or place of business without a firearms license.[9]

In my opinion, and that of many constitutional scholars, any and all gun control laws are unconstitutional, and therefore, should be nullified. The Second Amendment is every American's gun permit, and it shall not be infringed upon.

These three illegal and unconstitutional measures are part of a three-pronged approach to gun control that if left uncontested, could lead to confiscation and then extermination. Once Americans must register their firearms, they have lost a significant part of their Second Amendment rights. There is no longer anonymity with regard to gun ownership, thereby making it much easier for confiscation efforts.

History has shown us that those who force their citizens to register their firearms are more likely to have them confiscated. In many historical instances that is exactly what transpired shortly after registration.

In almost all scenarios throughout history, when the government confiscated the people's right to firearms they were eventually exterminated. One doesn't need to be a genius to understand that if you give up your guns you give up your freedoms and your right to defend yourselves and your families.

Now that we have clearly established that gun control throughout history is synonymous with genocides and extermination of political adversaries, we now must ask the fundamental question as to why then do our elected officials continue to push to disarm the public? Maybe that is a question that We the People might not like the answer to.

Gun-Free Zones Fill Up More Funeral Homes

Some of the numbers may vary, however, according to the Crime Prevention Research Center, as many as 92 percent of mass shootings occur in what are known as "Gun-Free Zones." A gun-free zone is typically a public area such as a school, library, church, movie theater, or restaurant that foolishly restricts the possession of firearms in their establishments.[10]

I bet that if you lined up ten criminals and asked them, "Would you rather commit your next crime in an area where the people are armed? Or would you rather commit your next crime in an area in which firearms are not allowed?" I am pretty sure we know the answer to that question.

Many Americans might think if we have fewer guns in society, it will make society safer. Sure, that and a peace rally, and we will all sleep safely at night. However, reality and facts speak otherwise. Every school shooting, post 1990, has one thing in common. They all happened in a gun-free zone. From Columbine to Virginia Tech and from Sandy Hook to Stoneman-Douglas, students and faculty have died because faculty were not allowed to carry a firearm on campus, and here is the main reason why.

Thirty-four years ago, back in 1990, when school shootings were on the rise, our lightbulb-bright members of Congress passed the Gun-Free School Zones Act, which made it unlawful to carry a firearm anywhere on school grounds.[11]

According to the Center for Homeland Defense and Security, (*security. org*) a total of 118 active shooter incidents have been reported at American schools since the Columbine shooting in 1999. These incidents happened in every age group ranging from kindergarten all the way through twelfth grade.[12]

What's even worse is that the same data also reveals that 440 people have been killed in those 118 shootings, and at least 1,243 have been injured! My prayers go out to every one of these victims and their families.

However, most people do not want to state and acknowledge the obvious, which is that all these people would still be alive today if they were not stuck in an unarmed school in a gun-free zone. Think of how many countless lives could have been saved if the people inside were able to exercise their Second Amendment right to self-defense?

Instead, 440 young, bright, amazing children's lives were destroyed before they even got started because they were gunned down due to gun-free zone laws. Moreover, it is not just schools in gun-free zones that are the problem. These areas are prevalent in almost every public area such as: restaurants, grocery stores, hospitals, churches, libraries, gyms, office buildings, arenas, etc.

Here are a few examples of shootings in gun-free zones:

1. Harvest Musical Festival in Las Vegas, Nevada
2. The Pulse Nightclub in Orlando, Florida
3. First Baptist Church, Sutherland Springs, Texas
4. Luby's Cafeteria, Killeen, Texas
5. Walmart Center, El Paso, Texas

6. Century Sixteen Movie Theater, Aurora, Colorado
7. Star Ballroom Dance Studio, Monterey Park, California
8. Inland Regional Center, San Berardino, California[13]

That was just eight mass shooting incidents in different and diverse areas. Imagine how many lives could have been saved if all these different types of public places allowed their patrons to carry a firearm? There is an old saying, "A good guy with a gun is the best way to stop a bad guy with a gun."

A Heller of a Better Idea

As stated previously, the Firearms Control Regulation Act banned the possession of a firearm in Washington, DC, but that rule was finally overturned by the United States Supreme Court in the Heller decision. The Heller decision, also known legally as *Heller vs. Washington, DC* was one of the most monumental decisions in regard to upholding the Second Amendment.

The case, brought to the highest court by police officer Dick Anthony Heller, challenged the constitutionality of the District of Columbia's strict gun control laws. Mr. Heller challenged the ruling that banned the possession of handguns in public places and private residences, as well as the requirement that all other firearms, including rifles and shotguns, be unloaded and even disassembled.

In a 5-4 decision, thankfully the Washington, DC gun law was ruled unconstitutional. The decision reaffirmed that the Second Amendment protects an individual's right to possess a firearm.

Another important aspect of the Heller decision was the court also added this line, "unconnected to service with a militia, and to use that firearm for traditionally lawful purposes, such as self-defense within the home."

This last part is very significant due to the numerous attempts by some politicians to argue that only those in a militia are allowed to own firearms. The Heller decision puts to rest any future challenges or ambiguity regarding the legitimacy of the militia argument.[14]

So here's my question. If the United States Supreme Court ruled that the District of Columbia's gun control law is unconstitutional, why are there still gun-free zones in Washington, DC or anyplace else in the country for that matter?

One would think that the Heller decision would have nullified all gun-free zones. Why haven't other cities around the country challenged their gun-free zone laws based on the legal precedent established by the Heller decision? There I go, asking questions again.

The uncomfortable truth is that more guns in the hands of law-abiding citizens makes society safer for everyone. The more guns the American people have and are allowed to carry freely, the less violent crime will be committed. Most criminals do not want to face armed resistance while in the process of committing a crime. They would rather strike where they know their victims are likely to be unarmed.

Besides, how many criminals do you know that follow the rules? The answer is zero. Why? Because they're criminals! The fact is that gun-free zones put countless more lives at risk then armed Americans walking around with a concealed weapon.

Which headline would you rather see? A crazed shooter runs into a school and shoots and kills twenty students and three faculty members. Or a crazed shooter runs into a school and is shot and killed by an armed teacher, saving countless lives in the process. I like the second one much better.

We Need More Guns in Schools to Make Them Safer

This is why Congress needs to introduce and pass what I will call the **Safer Schools Act**.

1. In order to stop school shootings, the first thing we need to do is repeal the Gun-Free School Zones Act, which will take the unnecessary target off these schools' backs.
2. Hire plainclothes armed officers to patrol the school and the grounds during school hours.
3. Hire teachers who have a firearms background or incentivize those willing to take a safety and self-defense course and sign a non-disclosure agreement that states they will not reveal to anyone else they are armed.

4. Install bulletproof glass on all the classroom doors and install a secret button under teachers' desks that can be pushed to automatically lock the doors and alert the police.
5. In more high crime areas, a police substation inside the school on campus may be necessary.

As far as the rest of society goes, the best way to make us safer would be to repeal all firearm laws, as every one of them is unconstitutional. In addition, we need to repeal all gun-free zones and allow more law-abiding citizens to carry firearms. If more Americans were carrying firearms in public places, the safer those places would be.

Activate the State Defense Forces

What are the State Defense Forces? SDFs, also known as state guards, state military reserves, or state militias, are state-level military units that are organized by individual state governments but remain separate from the National Guard.

State Defense Forces serve to provide each state with an extra layer of military force that can be mobilized at the behest of the state governor in response to national disasters, threats, emergencies, or specific state defense missions. In case you were wondering, yes, State Defense Forces are totally legal and even enshrined in our Constitution.

United States Title 32, Paragraph C, Section 109, under Maintenance of other Troops states, "In addition to the National Guard, if any, a State, The Commonwealth of Puerto Rico, the District of Columbia, Guam, or the Virgin Islands may, as provided by its laws, organize and maintain defense forces."[15]

Article I, Section 8, of the United States Constitution allows for the organizing, arming, and training of each state's militia retaining each state's rights to appoint and train the militia, thereby legitimizing the creation of state-based military forces. In addition, State Defense Forces are supplemented in their legitimacy by the Militia Act of 1903.

The Militia Act of 1903 fundamentally restructured the American militia system and ultimately established the framework for the creation of the National Guard. As of 2024, there are only twenty-one states including the

Commonwealth of Puerto Rico that currently have active State Defense Forces.[16]

The states with active and current State Defense Forces are:

1. Alabama
2. Alaska
3. California
4. Connecticut
5. Georgia
6. Indiana
7. Louisiana
8. Maryland
9. Massachusetts
10. Mississippi
11. Missouri
12. New York
13. Ohio
14. Oregon
15. South Carolina
16. Tennessee
17. Texas
18. Vermont
19. Virginia
20. Washington State
21. Puerto Rico (commonwealth)

State Defense Forces serve a variety of roles for each state and are separate from the National Guard in that they are purely state-controlled and cannot be federalized. Their members typically are made up of volunteers who assist the state during natural disasters and emergencies. However, what is most important to realize is that State Defense Forces are also used as a state's last line of defense against an overreaching and overbearing tyrannical government.

State Defense Forces and Our Constitutional Sheriffs

The Founders declared that the states were responsible for the nullification of unconstitutional laws. They understood that the people needed a way to protect their families and communities and looked to the sheriffs to organize their local defense forces.

Considering how so many politicians have abdicated their responsibilities and sheepishly followed whatever Washington, DC does, our constitutional sheriff's just might be our last and best line of defense.

If you live in a state that currently does not have an active State Defense Force, you are at a disadvantage. State Defense Forces cannot be federalized; therefore, they serve as a buffer between a potential federalized National Guard. Every state should have an active, well-funded, and highly trained State Defense Force in which to defend itself and its citizens.

If your state does not have an active State Defense Force, please consider **starting a petition** in your state and collecting enough signatures to introduce a ballot initiative, that if passed by the voters, would establish your state's Defense Forces. You can never have too many checks against the federal government's power.[17]

The Second Amendment is uniquely special to the United States, as it is enshrined in our Constitution as one of our most fundamental and important rights. Very few countries of the world allow their citizens to own and possess firearms.

The Second Amendment was not put in place for hunting or sport. It was created to allow freemen the right to self-defense and to protect themselves, their families, and their communities from invasion or illegal entry. Parenthetically, the Second Amendment's most important function is as a tool, which can be used to fight back against a tyrannical government, or a foreign or domestic threat.

What Our Founding Fathers Said about the Second Amendment

"That no man shall scruple, or hesitate a moment, to use arms in defense of so valuable a blessing, on which all the good and evil of life depends, is clearly my opinion."
—George Washington, letter to George Mason, April 5, 1769

"No free man shall ever be debarred from the use of arms. I prefer dangerous freedom over peaceful slavery. What country can preserve its liberties if their rulers are not warned from time to time that their people preserve the spirit of resistance. Let them take arms."
> —Thomas Jefferson, letter to James Madison,
> December 20, 1787

"Those that chose to give up essential liberty to obtain a little temporary safety deserve neither liberty nor safety. Democracy is two wolves and a lamb voting on what to have for lunch. Liberty is a well-armed lamb contesting the vote!"
> —Benjamin Franklin

"Besides the advantage of being armed, which Americans possess over the people of almost every other nation, the existence of subordinate governments, to which the people are attached, and by which the militia officers are appointed, forms a barrier against the enterprises of ambition, more insurmountable than any which a simple government of any form can admit of."
> —James Madison, *The Federalist Papers*, January 29, 1788

"Guard with jealous attention the public liberty. Suspect everyone who approaches that jewel. Unfortunately, nothing will preserve it but downright force. Whenever you give up that force, you are ruined. The great object is that every man be armed. Everyone who is able might have a gun."
> —Patrick Henry, Speech to the Virginia Ratifying
> Convention, June 5, 1778 [18]

Sadly, many Americans have been brainwashed into believing that if we just take away people's guns there will be less gun violence. The facts say otherwise. This may be hard for some people to grasp but the more guns in restaurants, bars, churches, concerts, etc. the safer those places will become.

We need more guns in society to make society safer, not fewer guns. As the great American writer Robert Heinlein once said, "an armed society is a more polite society."

CHAPTER SEVEN

Lab Leak or Wet Market? The Origins of Covid-19

For this chapter, I literally could fill an entire book by itself on everything I have researched, reported on, and exposed about the coronavirus in the last four years. Perhaps my second book will focus on all of it.

However, for the sake of time and covering other important topics, I will concentrate this chapter solely on Covid-19's origins and the subsequent cover-ups. As always, I will provide documented proof through emails obtained by FOIA requests and medical journals.

Not only will I show the cover-ups, but more importantly I will name names and expose the individual players and what their roles were. I will also shed some light into a very dark place where we find the real Dr. Anthony Fauci. We will discuss his role in all of this as well as some very shocking revelations and experiments that his National Institute of Allergy and Infectious Diseases (NIAID) was responsible for funding using your taxpayer dollars.

With that being said, I would not be true to myself if I didn't start out this chapter with these types of questions.

Was the coronavirus a meticulously planned worldwide event or just a coincidence? If it was planned, who planned it and why? Was it used as a new tool to control the world population and their movements? Or was the coronavirus a multitrillion-dollar worldwide money scam?

I know, I know, I should stop asking these types of questions. Maybe I should just plug my ears, put a blindfold on, and bury my head in the sand. I'm sure those who disagree with me will want me to just go away.

You might be thinking why is he asking those types of questions? Is he a Conspiracy Theorist? Being labeled a conspiracy theorist is typically what happens to people who question the official narratives of government and political officials, which I have made a successful career out of doing.

In case you were wondering, the term "conspiracy theorist" was invented in 1967 by the Central Intelligence Agency as a tool to discredit and marginalize anyone who did not agree with the official findings and narrative of the Warren Commission's Report on the Assassination of President John F. Kennedy.[1]

Ask yourselves this very important question.

Do you think it is possible that the United States government, along with the majority of the scientific community, in coordination with American and global media companies, worldwide organizations, world leaders, heads of state, pharmaceutical companies, supply chain companies, hospital administrators, Hollywood, public relation firms, and a multitude of other groups, could have collaborated on the creation of a worldwide pandemic?

Well, I'm sure you know by now, I don't do conspiracy theories. Covid-19 was not the result of a Wuhan meat market. Covid-19 was created at the Wuhan Institute of Virology in Wuhan, China, and it either accidentally escaped from the lab or was purposely released. Much more on that later.

What I can say with 100 percent accuracy is nothing is ever purely coincidental. Throughout my research, one thing is certain: after the pandemic officially ended, and people had time to reflect on the entire event, it raised many more questions than answers.

What Was Event 201? Who Attended It? What Was Its Alleged Purpose?

On October 18, 2019, the John Hopkins Center for Health Security, in partnership with the World Economic Forum, and the Bill and Melinda Gates Foundation, all sponsored an exercise officially known as Event 201.[2]

This exercise was allegedly designed to simulate what a potential future outbreak or pandemic may look like. The event also planned out and discussed different measures that would be needed in order to facilitate the navigation through any future pandemics. Before we get into Event 201 any further, let's give some background as to the three sponsors of this event.

The John Hopkins Center for Health Security

The John Hopkins Center for Health Security is an independent nonprofit organization affiliated with John Hopkins University School of Public Health. The center conducts research on emerging infectious diseases and epidemics. The center also is involved in preparedness training and response strategies.[3]

The World Economic Forum

The World Economic Forum, also known as the (WEF) is an international global organization that fortifies public and private cooperation through the engagement of political leaders, governments, corporations, and business leaders, in order to shape global, regional, and industry agendas.[4]

The World Economic Forum (WEF) in 2016, as part of their annual meeting of the Global Future Councils (*this sounds like something straight out of a Star Wars trilogy*), posted a video and blog post on their website.

The video was titled, "Eight predictions for the world in 2030," which discussed a future whereby owning property would be a thing of the past and you would be happy about it." The World Economic Forum sees a future world in which renting and communal sharing replaces individual property ownership.[5]

As I alluded to in a previous chapter, the World Economic Forum has also conducted extensive studies on developing alternative sources of protein and suggests that eating insects would provide a sustainable new source of protein. In addition, studies have also been conducted on the reuse of water, particularly wastewater for consumption. MMMM . . . bugs and sewer water, sounds delicious! Oh, thank you WEF!

The Bill & Melinda Gates Foundation

The Bill & Melinda Gates Foundation is a private foundation, founded by Microsoft founder Bill Gates. This foundation's main focus is on funding and creating new vaccines, creating and funding alternative food sources and supplies, and sustainable farming in nontraditional ways. Since when does a computer nerd suddenly become an expert on sustainable farming and creating vaccines without a background in medicine or agriculture?[6]

Shockingly, Farmer Bill is currently America's largest farmland owner with active farms under his ownership in as many as twenty states across the United States of America.[7]

Now that we have established the types of organizations that cosponsored Event 201, let's discuss the event itself in more detail. Event 201 was a three and a half hour long pandemic preparedness simulated exercise, whereby a series of dramatic, scenario-based, catastrophic events unfold around a new potentially deadly viral outbreak.

Moreover, Event 201 consisted of prerecorded news broadcasts, "live" staff briefings, and moderated discussions on specific topics. These issues were carefully crafted and designed to fit compelling narratives that educated the participants and the audience.

According to the exercise, it involved fifteen global business, government, and public health officials:

1. Latoya D. Abbott—senior director of Global Occupational Health for Marriott International
2. Sofia Borges—United Nations Foundation's senior vice president
3. **Brad Connett**—president of Henry Schein Medical Group, one of the largest manufacturers and distributors of medical equipment and supplies
4. Chris Elias—president of Global Development for The Bill & Melinda Gates Foundation
5. Timothy Evans—director and associate dean of Global Health at McGill University
6. **George F. Gao**—professor and the director-general of the Chinese Center for Disease Control and Prevention. The CCDCP is a

Chinese governmental organization that is under the control of the Chinese Communist Party.

7. **Avril Haines**—current US director of National Intelligence as well as former deputy director of the Central Intelligence Agency

8. Jane Halton—member of the Australian Strategic Policy Institute, and the chairwoman of the Coalition for Epidemic Preparedness Innovations

9. **Matthew Harrington**—chief operations officer at Edelman, the largest public relations firm in the world

10. Martin Knuchel—senior director of Crisis Management for Lufthansa Airlines

11. **Eduardo Martinez**—president of United Parcel Service (UPS) and responsible for overseeing over 440,000 UPS employees worldwide. He also currently serves on the World Economic Forum's Future Epidemic Steering Committee.

12. **Dr. Stephen Redd**—director of the Centers for Disease Control and Prevention's Office of Public Health Preparedness and Response

13. **Hasti Taghi**—media and communications professional, and former news anchor for CBS and NBC News. She currently serves as the vice president and chief of staff for the CEO at NBC Universal.

14. Lavan Thiru—Singaporean businessman and former government official.

15. **Dr. Adrian Thomas**—serves as the vice president for Global Health at Johnson & Johnson.[8]

Now, you may be wondering, why did I highlight eight out of fifteen of these individuals and what do they have to do with Covid-19? Other than the fact that they all attended an event together that simulated a future pandemic, maybe nothing; however, it is the industries they represent that raise more questions.

The attendees of Event 201 all possess unique and diverse backgrounds. Backgrounds you would come to expect if your goal was to protect people from a potential future global pandemic. However, was Event 201 really just a simple exercise on preparedness or something else?

Let's take a closer look at these four individuals first, in no particular order, that stand out for the industries which they represent.

Brad Connett, president of Schein Medical Group that provides a comprehensive range of medical supplies, including diagnostic and preventative products such as surgical equipment and supplies, pharmaceuticals, and vaccines.

Dr. Stephen Redd has lots of previous experience working with other global outbreaks such as H1N1, Ebola, and the Zika virus.

Dr. Adrian Thomas is a clinical Pharmacologist and vascular surgeon. He is also an expert on global health security threats, antimicrobial resistance, and multi-drug-resistant viruses.

Avril Haines has an extensive background in intelligence and government relations.

These four individuals on the surface might not set off any alarm bells, but it is interesting to point out the types of industries and agencies they come from. You have a doctor, who develops vaccines, and is in the pharmaceutical business.

Next you have another doctor who works for the CDC and has past experience with prior global outbreaks. After that, we have the current director of National Intelligence, who also worked for the Central Intelligence Agency, and the National Security Council.

Finally, we have an individual who is the president of one of the largest manufacturers and distributors of medical equipment and supplies.

I will admit, on the surface there is nothing wrong or nefarious about any of these individuals. However, if Event 201 was indeed just a simple exercise, as it had been promoted, then the timing of Event 201 must come into question.

Only four months after this exercise, the coronavirus pandemic hit the entire world. If this was a planned event, these industries and the agencies in which they represent stood to profit greatly from a global pandemic.

Now let's focus our attention on these next four individuals and see if they make you question their role in Event 201, and why they participated in it in the first place.

Matthew Harrington represents Edelman, which is a leading industry firm that partners with multiple businesses and organizations. Public relation firms are hired to develop, build, and sell messaging campaigns in order to shape public opinion. In addition, Edelman says on their own website, they're experts in protecting company reputations, promoting global brands, and shaping messaging campaigns.

Eduardo Martinez, president of UPS, has ties to the WEF and is also on the executive board of IMPACT 2030, which is a business-led coalition in partnership with the United Nations Sustainable Development Committee.

Hasti Taghi is a media and communications professional with ties to two mainstream media networks, CBS and NBC, as well as to the WEF.

George F. Gao has ties to at least three organizations and institutions that are tied to the Chinese Communist Party.

In addition, the Wuhan Institute of Virology where the coronavirus was created and leaked from is directly under the Chinese Academy of Sciences. This means that Dr. Gao, who is a professor of microbiology at the Chinese Academy of Sciences is directly affiliated with the Wuhan Institute of Virology!

So, Let's Unpack This, Shall We?

We have fifteen individuals, all with diverse backgrounds, who got together to discuss and "simulate" the next major global pandemic that just so happens to coincidentally hit America and the rest of the world only four short months later?

Fifteen individuals with backgrounds in: the intelligence community, the United States government, the Centers for Disease Control and Prevention, one of the largest pharmaceutical companies in Johnson & Johnson, the World Economic Forum, the Bill & Melinda Gates Foundation, the John Hopkins Center for Health Security, the United Nations, the United Parcel Service, and the World Health Organization.

Furthermore, the largest public relations firm in the world, one of the largest medical supply companies, a former news anchor who now is the vice president and chief of staff to the CEO of NBC News Universal, and an expert on diseases and viruses who is affiliated with the exact same laboratory in China that the virus originated from, and who is very likely a member of the Chinese Communist Party?

Nothing to see here, folks. I'm sure this is all just coincidental. Maybe I am just a conspiracy theorist after all. Or perhaps this event was indeed planned. What I do know for sure is we must never stop digging for the truth, and as one of my mentors, the late Barry Farber, would always say, "keep asking questions."

The Collusion and Coverup of the Scientific, Medical, and Governmental Communities on the Origins of the Coronavirus

Now that we have established the fact that Event 201 took place only four months before the Covid-19 pandemic hit, let's dig a little bit deeper into other aspects of what happened. It is important to note that as soon as Covid-19 reached a worldwide global pandemic status, the official narrative on the origins of the virus began to take shape.

This is when the majority of the scientific community, with the help of global media, social media, and governments around the globe, started to create a false narrative about the origins of the coronavirus.

The American scientific community, international and American media, the United States government, other world governments, the World Health Organization, Dr. Anthony Fauci (a lot more on him later), the National Institute of Health, the Centers for Disease Control and Prevention, the Food and Drug Administration, pharmaceutical company CEO's, and others collectively, and through careful coordination, came to a consensus narrative that the coronavirus's origins could be traced back to a natural occurrence at the Huanan Wet Market, in Wuhan, China.

A wet market is where merchants sell different kinds of fish and meats to the public. This is where they claim some type of animal, perhaps a pangolin, may have been infected with this new mysterious virus which, through natural means, spread from animals to humans.

This narrative was promulgated far and wide by all the news media outlets in America and around the world. Major social media companies like Facebook, Twitter, Instagram, and YouTube, all censored anyone on their platforms who said or posted anything different from the consensus narrative.

Suddenly, world-renowned scientists, virologists, infectious disease experts, and doctors were being censored or banned for daring to have an opposing view.

On a side note, the actions by these big social media platforms are one of the main reasons I am a supporter of repealing Section 230 of the Communications Decency Act. If this section of the CDA was ever repealed, it would allow users of these platforms, who were unceremoniously dismissed, banned, censored, and marginalized, the ability to sue these companies who violated their First Amendment right to free speech. Parenthetically, repealing Section 230 of the CDA would finally strip these companies of their protections against criminal and civil liability.

However, as I have stated previously in other chapters, facts are indeed stubborn things and Freedom of Information Act requests are perhaps the most stubborn of them all.

"Trust the Science"

International financial interests, as well as the global scientific medical establishment, never wanted the truth to come out about the origins of the coronavirus and went to great lengths to hide this information and the source of the outbreak. This was despite the fact that many in the scientific and medical communities initially suspected the origin of the virus to have come from the Wuhan lab.

I do not operate in vagueness or theories; I bring the receipts. The receipts in this case are documented proof through numerous pages of email communications between scientists, doctors, and government officials. These emails were obtained through (FOIA) Freedom of Information Act Requests.

According to these emails, the evidence shows that certain elements within the US government coordinated with select members of the US scientific community to continue the wet market narrative. Not only will I source everything I am saying, but I will do you one better. I will include each one of their email addresses as yet another layer of authenticity.

Some of the players involved, according to the email addresses are: Scientist Kristian G. Anderson (*KGA1978@gmail.com*) from the Scripps Research Institute, Ralph Baric (*rbaric@email.unc.edu*) from the University of North Carolina School of Public Health, Trevor Bedford (*trevor@bedford.io*) from the Fred Hutchinson Cancer Institute, Arivinda Chakravarti (*Arivinda.Chakravarti@nyulangone.org*) from the New York University School of Medicine, Peter Daszak (*daszak@ecohealthalliance.org*) from EcoHealth Alliance, and Gigi K. Gronvall (*ggronvall@jhu.edu*) from none other than John Hopkins School of Public Health, the EXACT same organization that was the main sponsor of Event 201![9,10]

By January 2020, there were already rumblings on social media platforms that were questioning the official wet market narrative. The most frightening part is that many in the United States scientific community not only knew the virus came from the Wuhan Institute of Virology, but even worse, had an active role in helping the Chinese government and the People's Liberation Army (PLA) develop the virus.

Specifically, through Ralph Baric's research at the University of North Carolina in cooperation with Peter Daszak's EcoHealth Alliance, and Dr. Anthony Fauci's NIAID, one of the organizations under the National Institute of Health (NIH) umbrella, all likely played a part in the creation of the virus. However, due to Big Tech censorship, much of this information was hidden from the general public.

It gets much worse. In February 2020, Kelvin Droegemeier, then director of the White House's Office of Science and Technology Policy (OSTP), wrote a letter to Dr. Marcia McNutt, who is the president of the National Academy of Sciences.

In his letter, he instructed the National Academy of Sciences, Engineering, and Medicine (NASEM) to immediately try to find information that would show the origins of the virus originated from "an evolutionary or structurally biological standpoint. *Translation*: figure out a way to show the origins of the virus originated in any way other than from the Wuhan lab.

Moreover, a majority of the scientists who were collaborators and consultants for the National Academy of Sciences have extensive histories working in concert with the Chinese Communist Party, and likely created the wet market narrative in order to release the Chinese from any culpability.

According to these email exchanges, one could make a strong case that the scientists involved in crafting the wet market narrative knew that the coronavirus likely originated from the Wuhan Institute of Virology lab.

Furthermore, perhaps due to financial rewards or gains or fear of losing million-dollar research grants, these scientists instead chose to protect the Chinese Communist Party while simultaneously protecting their own financial interests.

It is also a fact, through documentation, that Ralph Baric, from the University of North Carolina, had a long and documented history collaborating with Dr. Shi Zhengli, also known as "The Bat Lady."

Dr. Shi, who was one of the original scientists at the Wuhan Institute of Virology, and the virologist who was engaged in the dangerous practice known as gain-of-function research, which is the separation of the genome sequences of viruses to make them more virulent by splicing them until the virus is transmittable from animals to humans. Dr. Shi was working closely with American scientists who were funding and supporting this type of research.

George F. Gao Is Gao Fu, and a Likely Member of the Chinese Communist Party

Here is the craziest part yet. Remember George F. Gao? He was one of the fifteen attendees at Event 201. He is also either an official member of the Chinese Communist Party (*it is next to impossible to secure a high-level position such as the ones Gao has obtained without being a member*) or at the very least closely associated with them.[11]

According to a January 26, 2020, article written by investigative journalist Bill Gertz from the *Washington Times*, Gao Fu, the director of the Chinese Center for Disease Control and Prevention—wait a minute, I thought his name was George F. Gao?

A quick search online reveals that Gao Fu is also known as George F. Gao. Gao/Fu told Chinese state-run media that Covid-19 was part of a "United States conspiracy to spread germatic based weapons in an obvious attempt to deflect attention on China's own biological weapons program.[12]

Who is Dr. Shi Zhengli and Why Is She an Important Figure in the Lab Leak Theory?

Dr. Shi is a likely member of the Chinese Communist Party and a senior researcher at the Wuhan Institute of Virology. In 2014, she led a group of top researchers in a project that focused on splicing and splitting the gene sequences of horseshoe bats and coronaviruses.

As noted earlier, the project started as a joint research project. Principal researcher Ralph Baric from the University of North Carolina, Peter Daszak, president of EcoHealth Alliance, and Dr. Anthony Fauci, head of the NIAID all collaborated on these experiments, which took place under the supervision of Dr. Shi Zhengli at the Wuhan Institute of Virology.

The project was prominently featured in the article from *Nature Medicine* titled, "A SARS-like cluster of circulating bat coronaviruses shows potential for human emergence." The article was coauthored by fifteen researchers including Ralph Baric and Dr. Shi Zhengli.[13]

In 2014, the Department of Health and Human Services sent a letter to Ms. Sherrie Settle at the Office of Sponsored Research at the University of North Carolina stating the grant issued for research at the Wuhan laboratory "is being used to conduct gain-of-function research, and due to the risky nature of this research, we ask you to voluntarily pause the project immediately."

However, even though our government was no longer supporting this type of dangerous research, the Wuhan Institute of Virology continued the gain-of-function research and the project. The letter to Ms. Settle is on page sixty-four of these documents.[14]

The Two Peters

Other major players who had close ties to the Wuhan lab were Peter Daszak and Dr. Peter Hotez, professor of molecular virology at Baylor College of Medicine in Houston, Texas.

According to Dr. Richard Ebright, professor of chemical biology at Rutgers University, Dr. Peter Hotez funneled grants from 2016 until 2019 from the National Institute of Health (Grant ID AIO98775) to at least five separate research projects at the Wuhan Institute of Virology, and at least one was in collaboration with Dr. Shi Zhengli.

A 2023 *Vanity Fair* article titled "Secret warnings about Wuhan research predating the Pandemic" explains that in late October of 2017, US health officials with the National Institute of Allergy and Infectious Diseases (NIAID) arrived at the newly built Wuhan Institute of Virology. This was

China's first Biosafety-Level Four (BSL4) laboratory and research facility. BSL4 is the most dangerous level lab for experimenting on viruses.

The Wuhan Institute of Virology was funded in part by grants from American company EcoHealth Alliance for coronavirus research. Remember, all of this research and gain-of-function happened way before the pandemic started.[15]

The DEFUSE Project

According to a FOIA request from the nonprofit health advocacy and research group Right to Know, Peter Daszak proposed a project called the DEFUSE project.

This project's purpose was to genetically engineer and manipulate novel coronaviruses at the Wuhan Institute of Virology by taking horseshoe bats and introducing SARS-CoV-2 by inserting spike proteins in order to evaluate their propensity to infect humans through cell entry. In layman's terms, conducting gain-of-function research.

The grant proposal was submitted by Peter Daszak and EcoHealth Alliance to the Defense Advanced Research Projects Agency also known as DARPA, which is a secretive agency within the Pentagon that works on many different highly classified projects.

The best way I can think of to describe DARPA is like the fictitious agency that Will Smith and Tommy Lee Jones were a part of in the 1997 movie *Men in Black*. But, due to the extreme danger of this project, mainly the unintended consequences of a future pandemic, even DARPA refused the project, and it was eventually shut down.

However, just as the 2014 project by Ralph Baric and the University of North Carolina was shut down due to its dangerous nature, it didn't stop the scientists at the Wuhan Institute of Virology from advancing their own gain-of-function research, sadly taught to them by gullible American scientists.

Moreover, evidence shows that even though the Pentagon's DARPA agency refused the DEFUSE project, the technology and research was continued by the People's Liberation Army, which is part of the biological warfare team of Chinese scientists at the Wuhan Institute of Virology.[16]

Major Update on EcoHealth Alliance and President Peter Daszak

While in the process of writing this book and this chapter specifically, on May 15, 2024, the Department of Health and Human Services (HHS) suspended all future and current research grants of EcoHealth Alliance, effective immediately.

In addition, HHS has initiated debarment proceedings against Peter Daszak and EcoHealth Alliance due to the company's unethical, dangerous, and dishonest business practices. Daszak was caught lying to HHS and others about gain-of-function research and misappropriating research grants.

The decision comes from the Health and Human Services' own extensive investigation and the House of Representatives Select Subcommittee on the Coronavirus Pandemic. It focuses on the deep connections between EcoHealth Alliance and the Wuhan Institute of Virology.

The findings conclude that EcoHealth Alliance failed to adequately monitor and protect its research projects, as well as failed to provide essential documentation in regard to their research in connection with the Wuhan Institute of Virology.

One of the more serious and critical dangerous findings shows that Peter Daszak and EcoHealth Alliance on numerous occasions failed to adhere to strict guidelines regarding biosafety practices and requirements.

These serious infractions could have led to possible enhancement of viral pathogenicity or transmissibility through gain-of-function research, a practice that is currently under a moratorium in the United States.

Most troubling, the report concludes that the correspondence between Dr. Anthony Fauci's National Institute of Allergy and Infectious Diseases and Peter Daszak's EcoHealth Alliance showed that on multiple occasions research that was conducted did not meet the safety protocols and guidelines of research grant requirements.

According to Suspension and Debarment official H. Katrina Brisbon, "The findings and information in these records constitute adequate evidence to demonstrate that suspension and debarment of Ecohealth Alliance is necessary due to causes of a serious and compelling nature to which evidence is presented to demonstrate a need for immediate suspension in order to protect the public interest."

This is what you call a smoking gun, folks. Not only should Peter Daszak be debarred, and EcoHealth Alliance be defunded and shut down, but he should also be arrested for crimes against humanity and prosecuted to the fullest extent of the law for conducting illegal and dangerous gain-of-function research.[17]

Will the Real Dr. Fauci Please Fess Up?

Who is Dr. Anthony Fauci? To most Americans, he was the diminutive older gentleman either standing behind President Trump or speaking on his behalf as one of the so-called experts and leaders on the former president's Coronavirus Task Force.

The American people were fascinated with this sudden new face, even naming sandwiches and desserts after him. It was commonplace to see T-shirts, hats, mugs, buttons, etc. with his face on them. However, what the American people did not know then, and probably still don't know today about Dr. Anthony Fauci is his dark and sinister past.

Dr. Fauci, now retired, and as of this writing, still not prosecuted, had served as the Director of the National Institute of Allergy and Infectious Diseases (NIAID) since 1984. During his tenure, Dr. Fauci served under seven different presidents. The first president he served under was Ronald Reagan, then George H. Walker Bush, Bill Clinton, George W. Bush, Barack Obama, Donald Trump, and lastly Joe Biden.

Dr. Fauci's role throughout his long career had been as an advisor to the last seven presidents on outbreaks, public health emergencies, and infectious diseases. He has advised these presidents on health-related issues such as HIV/AIDS, SARS, H1N1, Ebola, Zika, and most notably the coronavirus.

He was one of the highest paid government officials during his long career. The carefully crafted and conducted public persona of Dr. Anthony Fauci is that of an innocent, diminutive grandfatherly type. A man, who seemed as if sent by God himself to rescue America and the rest of the world from the coronavirus, (that he helped fund).

However, when one digs a little deeper there are a lot of disturbing facts about the good doctor that the media and the medical establishment do not want you to know, including some emails, again discovered through one of those darn, irrefutable, pesky FOIA requests.

In a massive treasure trove of 3,234 emails, (many of which were redacted) from January 2020 to March 2020, Kristian G. Anderson from the Scripps Research Institute sent an email to Dr. Fauci in which *he admits the genome sequences of the virus and its features potentially looked to be engineered.*[18]

The facade around Dr. Fauci started to unravel after these emails were released. The emails show the lengths to which Dr. Fauci, his organizations, the scientific community, and many others went in order to protect one another.

In fact, federal records and emails released by the House Oversight Committee reveal that one of Dr. Fauci's top advisors even admitted that he used his personal email address to converse with his colleagues and his boss in order to circumvent any future Freedom of Information Act requests.

Dr. David Morens, who has served with Dr. Fauci for twenty-five years at the NIAID, wrote in an email released by the House Oversight Committee, "As you know, I try to always communicate on my Gmail account as my NIH email address is being constantly FOIA'd."

This is not only an incriminating statement and reference towards hiding information from the public record, but he even goes on to admit that "I will delete anything I do not want to see show up in The *New York Times.*"

Perhaps Dr. Morens is hiding something so dangerous and possibly illegal that he knows if it ever came to light, it would likely put him in legal jeopardy? These records can be subpoenaed by Congress, and I hope one day they will.[19]

Dr. Fauci's emails also show how he likely paid off Danish-born and British-educated scientist Kristian G. Anderson, who you will remember was part of the initial team of scientists who helped craft the consensus narrative that the coronavirus's origins came from the Wuhan Wet Markets.

Let's look at a timeline that shows Dr. Anthony Fauci's power and persuasion. On January 31, 2020, Kristian Anderson emailed Dr. Fauci stating, "Some of the features of this virus look to be engineered and the genome looks inconsistent with evolutionary theory."

Then only four days later, on February 4, 2020, after a long phone conversation with Dr. Fauci, Dr. Anderson did a complete 180 and said that the lab leak theory was nothing but a conspiracy theory. Kristian Anderson then says publicly, "The main crackpot theories going around at the moment related to this virus being somehow engineered are demonstrably false."

So, What Changed Kristian Anderson's Mind in Only Four Days?

Did Dr. Fauci put pressure on Kristian Anderson during that phone call in order to get him to change his story and do an about face on the lab leak theory? Did Dr. Fauci issue a threat to Kristian Anderson that if he did not change his opinion publicly, he would risk losing funding and grant money for future projects?

Well, as I always say on my show when I am looking for a motive, "follow the money." It is safe to say that financial rewards, payoffs, hush money, or even government grants can be highly effective motivating factors when you need someone to take a position they know is not the right one.

Dr. Andrew Huff is a whistleblower and the former vice president at EcoHealth Alliance. He is an epidemiologist and expert on infectious diseases. In 2022, Dr. Huff signed an official statement under penalty of perjury that stated, "I, Dr. Andrew Huff can attest that I analyzed the funding of Dr. Kristian G. Anderson, scientist with the Scripps Research Institute from data obtained from the National Institute of Health's funding database."

Dr. Huff continues, "The data shows that Dr. Anderson's funding increased from $393,000 monthly to $800,000 monthly after he changed his opinion on the lab leak theory." Dr. Anderson's funding dramatically increased after changing his position on the characterization of the agent as being man made, to naturally emerging, after a series of discussions with Dr. Anthony Fauci."[20]

Dr. Fauci Update: The Truth Is Finally Starting to Come Out.

According to a May 16, 2024, *New York Post* article titled, "We now know the likely truth about Covid, and how scientists lied." National Institute of Health deputy director Larry Tabak admitted that United States taxpayers funded gain-of-function research at the Wuhan Institute of Virology.

Game. Set. Match.

To think I laid out the entire coverup with emails from FOIA requests, medical articles, and emails and the National Institute of Health's deputy director validates everything I exposed in this chapter. Even when we catch them in their lies, they try to lie about that! Tabak tried to temper the seriousness of his admittance by saying, "Oh, gain-of-function research doesn't always mean what we have been told it means, it is perfectly safe."

As a result of the deputy director's comments, the National Institute of Health changed the definition of gain-of-function research to make it sound less dangerous and more benign. But I'm sure that is just another one of those coincidences, too.[21]

Six Foot Safe and Wear Those Masks!

Another MAJOR update that proves what a liar Dr. Anthony Fauci is, comes from his fourteen-hour private testimony in January 2024 in front of the House Select Subcommittee on the Coronavirus Pandemic.

During Dr. Fauci's testimony, he revealed two very important falsehoods that millions of people thought were true. Lord Fauci's recommendations were never questioned, and if you did so you were labeled as "anti-science." First, he admitted that the recommendations involving social distancing were not based on any particular study or even based in science.

According to the transcripts, Dr. Fauci was asked, "Did you see any studies that supported the six feet rule in reference to social distancing?" To which Dr. Fauci replied, "I was not aware of any studies, in fact, a study like that would be hard to do." So, essentially Dr. Fauci just admitted that the six feet social distancing rule was just made up!

In addition, Dr. Fauci has made several confusing and contradictory statements in regard to the effectiveness or ineffectiveness of wearing a face mask. During his testimony, once again he was noncommittal and vague. Dr. Fauci was asked, "Do you recall reviewing any studies or data supporting masking for children?" To which he replied, "You know I might have. I don't recall."[22]

Imagine that, millions of people around the country and the world feared being close to one another because Dr. Fauci said you could catch cooties? Then millions more covered their faces all because they were told that a piece of cloth would keep them safe?

Numerous studies have shown that children who were forced to wear face masks at school were less efficient and suffered learning and speech deficiencies. Millions of parents trusted this fraud, and their children suffered because of his edicts and recommendations.[23]

However, it is not just the coverups, the kickbacks, and the misinformation that make up the measure of this little man. It is the abhorrent and unethical treatment of animals and human beings that will also play a significant role in his tainted legacy. If the American people ever found out what I am going to expose here, they would be calling for Dr. Fauci's immediate prosecution.

Beagles, Monkeys, and Orphans, Oh My!

Part One: Beagles

I never thought I would need to put a disclaimer in any part of this book, however, due to the graphic details of this section, I must warn you what you are about to read is quite disturbing. Reader discretion is advised.

According to a Freedom of Information Act request on behalf of the White Coat Waste Project, which is a nonprofit advocacy group that aims to expose and end taxpayer funded animal experiments, Dr. Fauci is not going to receive any praise from PETA anytime soon.

These documents show that under Dr. Fauci's watch, over $375,800 of your tax dollars were commissioned to a study at a laboratory in the country of Tunisia. One of the torturous experiments was taking healthy beagle dogs, sedating them, then locking their heads into small mesh cages filled with hungry sand flies that would eat them alive. Before the experiment took place, NIAID admits that these beagles were put under anesthesia so scientists could perform vocal cordectomies so they suffered in silence.[24]

The study was focused around leishmaniasis, which is a parasitic disease found in Tunisia. The NIAID-supported study focused on infecting beagles with the disease in order to study the effects for a future vaccine. After these studies concluded, the beagles were euthanized.

Could you imagine the pain and suffering these poor dogs had to endure? Dr. Fauci should spend the rest of his life in jail for this alone. These flies were carrying a parasite that researchers wanted to study to see if the disease-carrying parasite could be transmissible to humans.[25]

There are a lot more evil, depraved, and disgusting details I could share with you all, however, I will refrain from doing so. Researchers even admitted that what they were doing was unnecessary as these same experimental drugs had previously been administered and tested successfully on laboratory mice and gerbils.

The research took place in September 2020 at the University of Georgia by Dr. Andrew Moorhead. Researchers admit that beagles were selected for this study in particular due to their sweet and trusting, tender nature.

These poor animals were tortured in these trials that lasted for three months! Sadly, it gets worse, at the end of the experiments the researchers euthanized every single beagle in order to study their infected blood for ways to see if the virus was transmissible to humans.[26]

Part Two: Monkeys

Here is another gruesome and cruel experiment uncovered by another Freedom of Information Act request by the investigators at White Coat Waste Project. The study took place in 2018 at the Yerkes National Primate Research Center at Emory University in Atlanta, Georgia.

Dr. Fauci's National Institute of Allergy and Infectious Diseases (NIAID) spent $16 million of your tax money torturing monkeys. This horrifying experiment consisted of drilling holes in their skulls and implanting head restraining devices on them. Then injecting the monkeys' brains with neurotoxins that destroy their brain causing them to lose control of their limbs, leaving most if not all eventually paralyzed.

As with the beagle experiments, there are many more vicious, cruel, and painful experiments and details I could share but again, for everyone's own sanity I will refrain from doing so. There were approximately four thousand primates at this facility that were used solely for these purposes. These Doctor Mengele type experiments on these animals are not only unnecessary and cruel but they were all funded under the watchful eye of Dr. Anthony Fauci.[27]

Part Three: Orphans

The Incarnation Children's Center located in New York City is the only pediatric skilled nursing facility that caters specifically toward children and adolescents from birth to age twenty-one years who are living with HIV/AIDS.

This hospital also has a long history of taking in orphan children whose parents have died from HIV/AIDS and passed it down to their children. These are the forgotten children who do not have any family to take care of them, and essentially, they become wards of the state. Sadly, these children are oftentimes neglected and exploited and treated like second-class citizens.

This is where Dr. Fauci and his associated research teams funded AIDS research drugs in 2004 on unsuspecting black orphans, most of whom were offered up by the hospital against their will.

These children were used as guinea pigs and experimented on with unproven, sometimes deadly drugs. Many of these drugs were forced into these children through nasal and gastric tubes. Researchers admit that these experimental drugs killed as many as two hundred children!

At the conclusion of these trials, the city of New York hired the VERA Institute, a nonprofit research and policy organization, to compile a final report on the drug trials. VERA was refused the medical records of the children used in the experiments, and none of the participants or their families were ever compensated.

The final report revealed that 25 children died before and during the drug trials, another 55 children died after the trials had concluded, and according to Tim Ross, former director of the Child Welfare program at VERA, 29 percent, or 121 children out of 417 children died within one year of the trial's conclusion.[28]

Sadly, these forgotten and tortured children were buried in a mass grave at the Gate of Heaven Cemetery in Hawthorne, New York according to research from the bestselling book, *The Real Anthony Fauci* by Robert F. Kennedy Jr.

So, let's recap who Dr. Anthony Fauci really is. Based on all the documents, emails, and funding grants from the NIAID and the NIH one could conclude, he is a liar, a coverup artist, an animal abuser, and a murderer.

This does not even take into consideration how many people died from the vaccines or his refusal to acknowledge that lifesaving drugs such as hydroxychloroquine and ivermectin would and could have saved hundreds of thousands, if not millions more lives.[29]

The War on Ivermectin and Hydroxychloroquine

So, why would Dr. Fauci discredit proven drugs like ivermectin and hydroxychloroquine, (*of which he was singing their praises during Ebola*) suddenly do an about face and say they are ineffective in treating Covid-19 when almost every single domestic and international study proves otherwise?

As I always say on my show, when something does not make logical sense, follow the money. It turns out that these two drugs are relatively inexpensive to administer. Remdesivir, on the other hand, costs upwards of $3,200 per treatment! Could it be that Dr. Fauci was getting either a kickback from Gilead or money from NIAID for co-funding the trials of the drug Remdesivir?

Not only did Dr. Fauci's National Institute of Allergy and Infectious Diseases co-fund the Gilead drug Remdesivir, but it was also partly developed at the University of North Carolina-Chapel Hill with professor of epidemiology Ralph Baric. You know, the same Ralph Baric who worked on gain-of-function research at the Wuhan Institute of Virology with the "bat lady" Dr. Shi Zhengli, but once again, I'm sure that is just another coincidence.[30]

The fact that Dr. Anthony Fauci has been allowed, at least for now, to escape justice and quietly retire with a $350,000 a year pension fully intact and not face criminal prosecution is a complete travesty of justice. Dr. Fauci was the highest paid government official, sometimes even topping the salaries of the president of the United States and top military officials.

To think this career politician, who lied about the origins of the coronavirus in order to protect his scientific community colleagues, is not being prosecuted for suppressing lifesaving drugs and treatments, covering up the lab leak origins, mercilessly torturing animals, and killing AIDS-infected orphans, is a prime example of a government official who is above the law.

As mentioned earlier, if more Americans read this and learned about who the true Dr. Anthony Fauci is, they would be calling for his prosecution. How this man, who doubled his income during the pandemic,[31] is still walking around as a free person is unconscionable. It is a slap in the face to every American and world citizen who died or was severely injured due to his actions.

Never forget, Dr. Fauci was a central figure in everything that went down in regard to Covid-19, and he should be held accountable for his role. Dr. Fauci knew that masks were ineffective, even contradicting himself on several occasions.

Dr. Fauci knew that lockdowns were psychologically damaging, especially to young children, but he went along with them anyway. In fact, the deprivation of people's rights through lockdowns is something psychologists and psychiatrists will be studying the effects of for many years to come.

Dr. Fauci admitted to the House Select Subcommitte on the Coronavirus Crisis that he knew masks were ineffective, that lockdowns did nothing to stop the spread of the virus as well as social distancing. In fact, he admitted to the Select Committee that the six feet rule was not based on science.[32]

Dr. Fauci used scare tactics and coercion to force our government to use illegal and unconstitutional mandates, and emergency use authorization rules to push a barely tested or even trialed experimental vaccine. For this alone he should be prosecuted for crimes against humanity at the International Criminal Court.

The number of people who are suffering from the side effects of these experimental vaccines is in the millions. Some of these side effects are permanent. Side effects such as: the rising rates of long Covid, sudden death increases, advanced cancers, early onset of dementia, sudden and severe strokes, pericarditis, myocarditis, severe blood clots, and more.

Dr. Anthony Fauci was the ringleader of the Covid-19 catastrophe. He, along with the heads of Pfizer, Moderna, Johnson & Johnson, AstraZeneca, and others need to be held accountable for their careless actions.

The lies, the cover ups, the payoffs, the cruelty, the waste, the danger, the evil. All of these topics leave more questions than answers. As I stated in the beginning of this chapter, there is enough material to write a separate book on this topic alone.

I believe when the history books are written, Dr. Anthony Fauci will go down as one of the world's most prolific mass murderers in history. He deserves to be stripped of his pensions, retirement, and license to practice medicine, and face prosecution.

CHAPTER EIGHT

The China Syndrome

"Victorious warriors win first and then go to war, while defeated warriors go to war first and then seek to win."[1] Those are the powerful words of Sun Tzu, the revered Chinese military general and strategist. The country of China has been perfecting the art of war against America since at least the 1970s when America foolishly started to legitimize China with their "ping-pong" diplomacy.

The phrase ping-pong diplomacy was born from the unexpected invitation extended by Chinese ping pong players to their American counterparts to visit China at the 31st World Table Tennis Championships in 1971.

American politicians saw this thinning of ice as an opportunity to leap headfirst into the Chinese market, ignoring their multitude of human rights abuses, and without a parachute. This gesture by the Chinese was the initial springing of the Red Dragon's trap, lying in wait patiently for America to fall right in.

Not soon after the ping-pong party, President Richard Nixon visited China, and by 1979, the United States and China signed their first bilateral trade agreement. This started a normalization of China and added legitimacy to a regime that was still killing political dissidents.

Did the American government demand the end of all human rights abuses before it would do business with China? Did the American government demand the end to political prosecution and imprisonment of Chinese dissidents before normalizing relations?

Of course not, instead they ignored these abuses and never held China accountable. Not only did they continue to do business with China, but they even legitimized an evil regime in favor of cheap products and even cheaper labor.

Sun Tzu also said, "He who is prudent lying in wait for their enemies when their enemies are not, will be victorious."[2] One of the greatest traits most Communists possess is patience. Judging by the looks of things today, China has been lying in wait for many years.

If you need any more proof of whether or not Nixon's ping-pong diplomacy has worked well for China at the expense of America, look no further than these iconic American companies that are, well, not very American anymore.

1. General Electric—One of the most iconic companies in American History has sold its appliance division to the Haier Group in Qingdao, China. In 2016, Haier purchased the division for $5.6 billion dollars.[3]
2. Radio Flyer—Not the red wagon! Yup, one of the most iconic American toy brands in American history is now mostly manufactured in China since 2004.[4]
3. Hoover Vacuums—One of the most recognizable brands of vacuum cleaners was founded in Ohio in 1908. Now it is owned by Techtronic Industries from China.
4. General Motors—Can you think of a more American brand? While not entirely owned by China, since 1998, General Motors has been in partnership with the Shanghai Automotive Industry Corporation (SAIC).
5. The Waldorf-Astoria Hotel—This iconic hotel is not just one of the most famous luxury hotels in Manhattan, it is an institution. However, in 2014, it was purchased by the Anbang Insurance Group in China.
6. Barbie Dolls—Ask any American girl in the last fifty years, and she can tell you her favorite Barbie Doll. In 1997, Mattel, Inc. moved the majority of their manufacturing to China where the dolls are now produced.

7. Craftsman Tools—This company's slogan was confidently "Made in America, Guaranteed Forever" Well, forever came and went because Craftsman Tools are now manufactured by APEX Tool Company with headquarters in China.
8. Black and Decker—A Maryland, USA-based company, has been in business in America for close to one hundred seventy-five years. However, the company now has some of its manufacturing in China.
9. American Eagle Outfitters—I put this one on the list mainly due to the irony of the brand. The brand now has manufacturing plants in China.
10. Rawlings Inc.—What's more American than a beautiful leather Rawlings baseball mitt? Apparently, not much these days due to a large portion of their products being manufactured in China.[5]

Sadly, this is only the tip of the iceberg. There are many more companies that started in America and now manufacture their products in China. Those products are scattered through the majority of American homes. If you want to see the magnitude of China's influence on our lives, may I suggest playing the Made in China game.

All you need to do to play is walk into any room in your house and pick up ten different items. The likelihood of all or some of those items being made in China is very high. If you find a lot of products made in China, throw them out and replace them with products made in the USA, or at least any other country but China.

Sun Tzu also said this, "I can think of no time in history where a nation benefits from prolonged warfare."[6] This is not only a true statement, but it is happening to America and most of us do not even realize it. Make no mistake about it, China has been performing prolonged warfare on the United States for decades. Americans, whether they know it or not, are at war with China, it just has not been formally declared.

Let's start with what most national security experts would agree upon, that China and the Chinese Communist Party (CCP), along with their secretive military apparatus, which is run by the People's Liberation Army (PLA), present the greatest existential threat to the safety and security of the United States of America.

China's currency manipulation, their unfair trade practices, and their refusal to abide by the international community on a whole host of issues, are some of the reasons why China will be America's greatest political and military challenge of this century.

China presents the most complicated and multi-faceted set of dangers that puts them in a class all by themselves. From their sophisticated spying networks to their highly organized cyber warfare practices, they present a clear and present danger to our national security and our infrastructure.

As we learned in the last chapter, China not only created the coronavirus in the lab using dangerous gain-of-function research, but it is continuing this work today. The Wuhan Institute of Virology is not just a simple research facility working on ways to prevent outbreaks and pandemic; it is China's biological weapons playground as well.

Was Covid-19 just a test run for a more serious and deadly outbreak or future pandemic? What is America and the international community doing to stop China's biological warfare ambitions? When could the next virus be released? These are the terrifying questions America must be demanding the answers to.

Social Distancing till Death

As draconian as the measures were in America and other countries around the world, no country treated its people quite as harsh as China. CCP chairman Xi Jinping's "zero covid policy" led to countless deaths.

In the earliest days of the outbreak, CCP officials would travel to highrise apartments in Wuhan and the surrounding cities. Government Officials would then go door to door and force the occupants to answer.

Once the people inside opened their doors, they were forced to have their temperatures taken. If they registered a high enough temperature they were then welded into their homes to "social distance" until they were dead.[7]

Many eyewitnesses who managed to escape came back many weeks later to the horrible smell of decaying bodies. It was even reported by surviving Wuhan citizens that they witnessed middle of the night fires burning behind Wuhan's largest mortuary.

With hospitals, morgues, and funeral homes overwhelmed and with overcrowding and a shortage of hospital beds, the Chinese government resorted to these inhumane types of practices. Due to China's secrecy, it is very difficult to know just how many people died or were likely killed by the Chinese government's strict and deadly Covid measures. What we can say for sure is that whatever number they reported, double or even triple it for good measure.[8]

Eye See You

China's draconian social credit scoring system shows just how little respect they have for their citizens. Initially proposed back in 2007, China's social credit scoring system was launched in 2014 with a goal to "score" every Chinese citizen based on their respect, loyalty, and above all else, trust level to the Chinese Communist Party.

China wants obedient, trusting citizens who don't question authority or speak until spoken too. They want citizens who support the Communist Party above all else. Social credit scores are the Communist Party's main tool to control the people and force them to be obedient.

Every Chinese citizen is placed in a digital database that stores all of their personal information. They are then "scored" by the Chinese government based on the level of admiration or discontent they show towards the government.

In addition, they are also scored on their personal behaviors and habits. Do they smoke or drink? Do they gamble or steal? Do they go out of their way to praise the Chinese Communist Party on a daily basis?

These, and many other factors, will determine whether or not some Chinese people will have a tougher life with fewer privileges than others, or an easier life full of opportunity and privilege. It all depends on whether or not an individual lives their lives to the standards and expectations of the Chinese Communist Party.

If you are a good little Communist and the government believes you to be trustworthy, then you will get perks, praises, and rewards. These can include preferential treatment in regard to securing credit and loans, easier acceptance to colleges and universities, and even better paying jobs.

If you dare to think for yourself, you will likely receive very low scores. You may not be able to gain access to fly or to ride on high-speed trains. You won't be able to even apply at some schools and private universities. You might not even have access to the internet or slow bandwidth. But worst of all, you will be publicly shamed on billboards showing your scores!

This is how China controls its people's every action. They financially incentivize the behavior they want and defund the behavior they don't. Many fear that its successful implementation could serve as a model for other authoritarian regimes throughout the world to follow.

China's Belt and Road Initiative and Debt Trap Diplomacy

What is debt trap diplomacy? Sounds like something used to trick people, doesn't it? The term refers to a powerful lending country, in this case China, purposely extending significant amounts of credit and capital to impoverished nations so they can build infrastructure such as airports, train stations, schools, and hospitals.

However, there's just one catch. China lends them this money with the knowledge that the country they are lending to will never be able to pay them back. So why would China build up a poor country's infrastructure?

Certainly, it is not from the goodness of their hearts. If they were genuinely concerned for people's well-being they would not currently have over one million Uyghur Muslims in forced labor and concentration camps. More on this a little later in this chapter.

So, why then are they doing it? As part of China's goal for world domination they leverage these debts these countries owe them into political favors or concessions. Perhaps they need a critical vote to pass on an important issue. They can write off some of the debt in exchange for their vote.

Perhaps China is also using these debts to get other countries to ignore China's human rights abuses by forgiving some of their debt in exchange for their cooperation, however, the main reason is likely even more sinister.

China likely uses debt trap diplomacy to control the governments of the countries that are indebted to them. This is how China uses debt forgiveness to buy off politicians, judges, and even whole governments.

This is all part of a sinister plan for world domination called the Belt and Road Initiative. Developed in 2013, BRI is a massive infrastructure and economic development project that as of 2021 has agreements and projects in over one hundred and forty countries. This makes BRI one of the world's largest international economic and social development projects of the twenty-first century.[9]

Everybody Wants to Rule the World
Okay, maybe I'm dating myself here. In 1985, British pop band Tears for Fears wrote a song titled, "Everybody Wants to Rule the World." Fast forward to the present day and that song could be China's new anthem if not their direct objective.

China's aggressive posturing towards Taiwan could turn the South China Sea into another dangerous warzone involving our allies and an unpredictable North Korea.

China's aggressive expansion in the South China Sea represents another significant threat to regional stability, especially towards western allies such as Japan and South Korea.

China's buildup of military installations and artificial islands in disputed waters and territories poses an immediate and constant threat to the safety, security, and sovereignty of other countries in the region.

Over a third of all global shipping passes through the South China Sea including oil and natural gas, which is almost 80 percent of Japan and South Korea's total imports. China's militarization includes: the deployment of missile delivery systems, radar technology, even several fleets of fighter jets patrolling the waters has increased tensions in the area.

Any major conflict or disruption in these contested waters could have devastating global economic implications for every country in the world, including the United States. With so much of the world's trade going through these waters, any prolonged conflict in the South China Sea would have far reaching implications for the world's economy.

Follow the Red Balloons
Let me date myself again. Growing up as a child in the 1980s, there was a French movie from 1956 called, *The Red Balloon*. It was a story about an eight-year-old little boy named Pascal, who follows a red balloon through the streets of Paris, France.

China's spy balloon program, part of its broader cyber warfare and surveillance apparatus, presents an opportunity for China to gather intelligence on America's landscape, infrastructure, and military bases and installations.

You may remember numerous instances in 2023 of these sophisticated high-altitude balloons traversing American airspace. The primary intelligence these balloons gather includes signal intelligence (SIGINT) which allows these balloons to intercept communications between different types of devices.

In addition, these balloons are equipped to record and even disrupt electronic communications (ELINT) to jam signals or record and capture military communications and movements, thus allowing China an overview of America's military capabilities, giving them a strategic advantage and competitive edge in geopolitical maneuvering.[10]

So, now that we understand the grave threat America faces from China, what can we as concerned Americans do to stop them? Well, the answer is not that complicated, but it could be very unpopular.

Short-Term Pain for Long-Term Gain

Are you a proud American who is willing to pay a little more in the short term for products not made in China? If you love your country and want more American businesses to flourish and compete, you likely are.

China is the United States' second largest holder of our national debt. As of the first quarter of 2024, China holds approximately $860 billion dollars or 10.2 percent of our national debt. By some estimations, the Walmart Corporation accounts for more than one percent of China's total US imports.

Big box stores, like Walmart and Target, are part of the problem. Target imports roughly 34 percent and Walmart imports roughly 26 percent of the products they sell directly from China.

There are some positive developments though, as Walmart has started to shift its imports away from China and instead to India. By diversifying their imports away from China, India is aligning with a broader geopolitical strategy of which the goal is to hopefully encourage more American companies to consider diversifying their imports away from China as well.[11]

One of the motivating factors that made Walmart and other big corporations start to diversify their imports was President Trump's tariffs on Chinese goods. The Trump administration placed a 25 percent tariff on $200 billion worth of Chinese goods. This forced many large American companies to rethink their import strategies and trading partners, many of which smartly moved away from China.

Made in the PRC
Also, please do not be fooled by China's latest marketing trick, "Made in the PRC." This may sound to the average American consumer as having nothing to do with China, but it certainly does. You see, because of people like me who have been calling for boycotts on all Chinese-made products, the Chinese government has gotten smarter.

Instead of using Made in China on all their manufacturing labels, they are starting to use Made in the PRC. What is the PRC you might be wondering? It stands for the People's Republic of China or the old-fashioned way of saying it, Made in China.[12]

Well, if it took the use of tariffs to force retailers to import their products from any other place but China, we Americans now must do our part. If every American consumer took the time to read and watch labels prior to making purchases it would be a good start.

If more Americans refused to buy products made in China or the PRC, we could gain our competitive advantage back by allowing more small businesses to thrive, thus creating more American jobs in the process.

TikTok Is Not Just a Social Media App, It's Chinese Spyware
In the last few years, the popular social media app TikTok has exploded in popularity. With over a billion daily users, TikTok is now the fifth largest social media app especially popular with teenagers, who are impressionable and vulnerable to TikTok's American-based algorithms.

According to a 2022 report from the Center for Countering Digital Hate, TikTok pushes harmful content towards its teenage users, who at that age already may have body positivity issues, such as encouraging eating disorders and self-harm into user's feeds, even as soon as they create the account!

According to the study, two-thirds of teenagers actively use TikTok, and the average user spends roughly eighty minutes a day on the app. For this study, researchers set up new accounts in the United States, United Kingdom, Canada, and Australia, at the minimum age TikTok allows its users, which is thirteen. Next, the accounts paused on videos about body image (but not bulimia or anorexia) and mental health issues such as anxiety and depression (but not suicide).

It took TikTok's algorithm a little over two minutes to start recommending different videos about suicide! Moreover, within eight minutes TikTok's algorithm started to recommend videos about bulimia, anorexia, how to stick your finger down your throat, where to buy baggy clothes, etc.

If you are reading this, and like myself have children, this is your worst nightmare. Imagine that, a social media app that purposely shows your son or daughter content that not only encourages the behavior you are trying to stop or treat, but more importantly, exacerbates the problem.

Our number one goal as parents is to use every resource at our disposal to protect our children. When our children need help and are struggling with something, we help them, we encourage them, we listen to them, and we try to fix whatever the issue may be as soon as possible and as best we can. We don't expect nor deserve a social media app trying to undermine our efforts and harm our children!

So why then is TikTok purposely exposing harmful content to our children? Well, the title of the article in which the study took place was called, "Deadly by Design." Clearly it seems as though TikTok's algorithms were intentionally set to target western children.[13]

TikTok is owned by a Chinese company called ByteDance. ByteDance was founded by Chinese tech expert Zhang Yiming. Like all wealthy Chinese entrepreneurs, it is next to impossible to know whether someone is an active or former member of the Chinese Communist Party.

However, as I have stated previously in other chapters, it is also next to impossible for wealthy Chinese business and political leaders to be in their positions without being a loyal member of the Chinese Communist Party.

Zhang Yiming is an only child and son of two civil servants, which is likely a nicer, more deceptive way of saying Chinese government officials. Yiming also went to Nankai University in Tianjin where he studied micro-electronics and software engineering. Nankai University is a state run and operated public university that is part of the Communist Party's Ministry of Education.

The National Radio and Television Administration, (sounds like some Hollywood organization but it's not) NRTA, is the state-controlled propaganda ministry of the Chinese Communist Party that helps implement the teachings of the party's ideology to all students. Zhang Yiming had to issue a formal apology to NRTA because ByteDance was not using enough propaganda to suit the Chinese Communist Party's corporate philosophy centered around the "Socialist Core Values" and promoted by Chinese Communist Party leader Xi Jinping, and promised "greater cooperation" to promote the Party's core values on the app.[14]

I Spy a Social Media App

The United States Intelligence Community has long deemed TikTok/ByteDance a national security threat and claims the app's users are at risk of being surveilled by the Chinese government, which owns a large percentage of TikTok's parent company, ByteDance.

An explosive multifaceted 2023 investigation by Forbes.com, which affirms Congress's own separate investigation into the social media app, found that TikTok users and creators' personal information, including their names, personal addresses, their financial information, even their social security numbers, are all stored on servers in China.

TikTok/ByteDance refuses to say how many individuals at the two companies have access to users and creators' personal information, their financial information, or who exactly has access to this information. Moreover, TikTok/ByteDance also refused to answer where in China this information is being stored and for what purpose.[15]

Bottom line, if your son or daughter or grandchildren are using TikTok it would be in their best interest to block it on their phones. This app is a proven national security risk and therefore it should be treated as such. Sorry kids, but we parents know what is best for you, and TikTok is not good for your mental or psychical health.

TEMU, Pinduoduo, and PDD Holdings

Anybody who has ever watched my show on a regular basis will know I am no fan of the Chinese Communist government. They have attacked me personally on numerous occasions, causing thousands upon thousands of dollars in repairing cyber-attacks, DDOS attacks, simultaneous multiple location attacks, you name it. There's a reason I am up to my fifteenth level of security on my website.

However, enough about that. Let's dive into another moneymaking scam called TEMU that China is pulling off that is making them billions. The name TEMU stands for Whaleco Technology Limited, which is operated by the Chinese e-commerce company Pinduoduo Incorporated. PDD Holdings, as it is more commonly known in the business world, has a very checkered past.

In September 2022, PDD Holdings, the parent company of TEMU, was launched in Shanghai, China. In 2023, less than a year later, PDD Holdings (in a possible attempt to mask its founding) changed its legal domicile from Shanghai, China to Dublin, Ireland and here is the likely reason why.[16]

Imitations, Knockoffs, and Piracy
In April 2019, PDD Holdings was named to the Office of the United States Trade Representative's List of Notorious Markets for Counterfeit Products and Piracy. Wow, that was a mouthful.

In 2018, PDD Holdings admitted to selling counterfeit products, and responded by closing 1,128 stores. In addition, they were also forced to remove as many as four hundred thousand counterfeit listings.

The company also disclosed that it removed an additional five hundred thousand counterfeit substandard medical equipment items, in particular imitation face masks in February 2020.

In 2023, even Google had seen enough and removed Pinduoduo's app from the Play Store after a Chinese cyber security firm found embedded malware in the app. Two days after the app was removed, Pinduoduo disbanded their team of engineers and project managers, likely in an effort to protect them from culpability, and transferred much of the team over to, you guessed it, TEMU, where they could continue working in various departments.[17]

TEMU Should Stand for "The Exploitation of Muslim Uyghurs"
If TEMU'S only problem was selling counterfeit items, that would be bad enough; however, who is making their products is where the true horror

story begins. The Chinese Government has had contention with ethnic Muslims in the Xinjiang region of far west China, known as Xinjiang Uyghur Autonomous Region or XUAR, for many years.

In 2014, China suffered a series of random attacks, including the Kunming Railway Station stabbing by a group of eight ethnic terrorists. The attackers, who were armed with long-bladed knives, randomly attacked and killed thirty-one people and injured another one hundred and forty more.

In response to these and other random attacks, Chinese Communist Party Leader Xi Jinping announced the "Strike Hard Campaign Against Violent Terrorism" which in turn led to the eventual internment of more than one million Uyghur Muslims in concentration, re-education, and forced labor camps by 2017. The worst practices of twentieth-century totalitarianism had once again reared its ugly head.

Since 2009, according to a Department of Labor press release titled, "Against their will: The situation in Xinjiang," China has been included on the list of goods produced by Child Labor or Forced Labor List (TVPRA). It is estimated that well over one hundred thousand Uyghur Muslims are working in forced labor camps today.[18]

One of those camps, masquerading as a "vocational and training" center, is the Wensu County Vocational Skills, Education and Training Center in Xinjiang, China, which is in the Uyghur Autonomous Region.

This is where the detainees of this facility are taught how to make wigs, costumes, tailoring, carpet weaving, clothing, baking, cooking, electronics production, electronics repair, automotive production, automotive repair, and much more.

According to multiple sources, including the Department of Labor, Bloomberg News, Federal Newswire, the BBC, the *New York Times*, and many others, TEMU sells products made by detainees in forced labor camps in the Xinjiang region.[19,20,21,22]

Things have gotten so bad that a bipartisan bill by Republican Senator Marco Rubio and Democrat Senator Jeff Merkley introduced the Uyghur Forced Labor Prevention Act (UFLPA) which was signed into law in 2021.

The law requires the United States Department of Homeland Security to block imports from the Xinjiang region that employs slave labor of Uyghur Muslims by adding to a restriction list of manufacturers, exporters, and other violators. This law was supposed to protect the Uyghurs against forced labor, but clearly these practices are still being continued.[23]

America, Please STOP Shopping On TEMU!

According to an April 2024 report in Yahoo Finance, the TEMU app has skyrocketed up to number one most downloaded e-commerce app, surpassing Amazon, Target, and Walmart. This is remarkable in the sense that this company is barely even a few years old and already is taking a considerable market share away from much more established e-commerce companies.

In December 2023, Reuters reported that TEMU was successfully challenging some of the bigger stores that unfortunately also sell a lot of Chinese-made products such as Dollar Tree and Dollar General, which account for 28 percent and 43 percent of the American market share respectively. Even Amazon has been affected by the rise of TEMU as they recently laid off 5 percent of their "Buy with Prime" workforce.

However, the company that so far has suffered the most is the 99 Cent Only stores. The company announced earlier this year that due to changing consumer demands and economic challenges they will be closing all 371 locations in Arizona, California, Nevada, and Texas. It is estimated that due to these closures, as many as 14,000 people will lose their jobs.[24]

So, how do you think TEMU can sell products online for half price and sometimes even 75 percent less than their closest competitor? The answer is they have ZERO payroll costs! The Uyghurs are being forced to make TEMU'S items for free in forced labor camps!

So, let's recap, shall we?

TEMU is a relatively new e-commerce company, whose parent company PDD Holdings and Pinduoduo had been forced to admit in the past that the company has sold hundreds of thousands of counterfeit products that were all likely made in forced labor camps by ethnic Uyghur Muslims.

Moreover, this shady new company has fooled the American consumer to the tune of 17 percent market share, which in turn has already put one major company (99 Cents Only Stores) out of business. Also, another competitor, Dollar Tree Inc., has announced they plan on closing one thousand of their stores in the near future.

Every time American consumers shop on TEMU, they are likely supporting forced labor! So please, for your own conscience and love of humanity, stop buying items from TEMU and instead buy American!

As I have stated previously, I have been targeted by the CCP in the past, and I have no doubt after this book comes out, I will likely be targeted by the CCP again. That's okay because somebody must be brave enough to say this. Americans must be educated about these things so we can decouple from China and weaken their regime.

How You Can Help Financially Weaken the Chinese Communist Party

As Americans, we must understand that the more we purchase Chinese-made products the more money we are generating for their war machine. Every time Americans purchase goods made by China, they are unknowingly financing their own demise as much of those profits go toward building up China's military.

Assuming we have a different president in the next few months with a new administration and a new congress, we must push to reinstate tariffs on all Chinese-made or PRC imported goods; however, even that might not be enough.

Congress Needs to Introduce the Rein-In China Competitive Advantage Act.

First, they will have to create it because I just made up this next part right now. If I was introducing this as new legislation it might go something like this:

Any company or corporation that sells Chinese-made products in the United States or its territories will be required to pay an extra 50 percent tax on all imports from any region in China. This would be, of course, on top of any extra costs on shipping fees as well.

The goal of legislation like this would be for disincentivizing American companies and consumers from purchasing Chinese-made products. In addition, in order for a retailer to sell Chinese-made products, American companies would be required to separate those products and clearly label, list, and display them separately from products made and manufactured in the USA or other countries.

If more American consumers had a better knowledge of where products they were purchasing were made, they likely would choose to purchase products made in the USA or another country other than China; even if those products were more expensive.

Americans must change their buying and spending habits and think about the consequences of buying Chinese-made products. The American consumer must ask themselves, is it worth it to prop up America's biggest existential threat just to save a few bucks on inferior products?

With every purchase of Chinese-made goods, the American consumer is funding another cyberattack against us, another balloon invasion recording our military installments, another anti-American social media app targeting our children, or worst of all, another lab-grown virus that could be even more deadly than the last one.

Buying American-made products is easier than you think. One way to avoid buying Chinese-made products is to stop shopping at Walmart and Target for starters. There are many online websites where you can purchase American-made products and I listed some of them below.

A List of Made in the USA E-Commerce Websites

1. www.madeinamericastore.com
2. www.authenticity50.com
3. www.madeintheusa.com
4. www.allamericanclothing.com
5. www.americanmademan.com
6. www.madeinusaproduct.com
7. www.usamade1.com
8. www.americanmanufacturing.org
9. www.themadeinamericamovement.com
10. www.usalovelist.com

It is important to always do your own due diligence and investigate every product, claim, company, and manufacturer. There are even some apps you can download on your phone that will allow you to input the barcode for the manufacturing location. One such app is called Made In. Another popular choice is barcodelookup.com

Sun Tsu says, "The opportunity to secure ourselves against defeat lies within our own hands. But the opportunity to defeat our enemies is provided by our enemies themselves."[25] If Americans can finally understand the threat that China presents to every American, they will then have the tools necessary to finally defeat the Chinese Communist Party.

CHAPTER NINE

The Class Warfare Argument and Universal Basic Income

If you take from the rich, you give the rich less incentive. If you give what you have taken from the rich to the poor, you make the poor more dependent, nobody wins. That is an original quote I thought of years ago when I first approached this issue.[1]

Richard Cloward and Francis Fox Piven were two sociology professors at Columbia University, who in 1966 wrote an article in the magazine *The Nation* titled, "The Weight of the Poor: A Strategy to End Poverty."

Instead of helping poor Americans by advocating for more funding for vocational training or skill development, these two professors wanted to create more poverty. Their stated goal was to precipitate an artificial crisis through the mass enrollment of poor Americans onto the welfare rolls with the stated goal of overloading and overwhelming the country's financial system.

Cloward and Piven's objective was to create a crisis by exceeding the system's capacity to meet these new demands by generating more dependency on the federal government, with the hopes of forcing politicians and policy makers to enact new legislation to address the perceived inadequacies within the welfare system.

Their hope was that with millions more receiving benefits, it would lead to more distribution of wealth and to the implementation of a guaranteed income. In other words, keep the people impoverished by keeping them dependent on the government.[2]

What a shocker! Two sociology professors that are also socialists. I guess Cloward and Piven never heard of the "makers versus takers" argument, which we will get into a little later on in this chapter. There are currently about forty-one million Americans currently on welfare already, which constitutes about 13 percent of the entire population.[3]

One could argue that a form of the Cloward and Piven strategy is being implemented in some capacity right now. Although there are supposed to be restrictions on illegal immigrants receiving benefits, many states do not enforce these laws. With our open borders policies, many new immigrants are receiving benefits such as food assistance, luxury housing, free education, free diapers, driver licenses, and even voter identification cards. Seems as though the Cloward and Piven strategy is working just fine.

Whether one calls it redistribution of wealth, a minimum guaranteed income, or universal basic income, it is not income, it is theft. Theft from tax paying hard working Americans who are subsidizing those Americans who rely on these workers for their benefits.

Thomas Jefferson once famously said, "A government large enough to give you everything is also large enough to take everything from you." Jefferson understood the dangers of big government and tried to warn his fellow Americans that those benefits you are receiving indeed do come with a price, your liberty and your freedoms.[4]

One of the biggest consequences of a city or state supplying no strings attached money to their constituents is disincentivizing people to work. This in turn creates more long-term dependency and laziness. America's national debt is already a staggering thirty-four trillion dollars. Handing out hundreds or even thousands of dollars per month in no strings attached income just exacerbates the problem.

Another unintended consequence of guaranteed income is a shortage of the labor force. The more people that are not working, the more government dependency. The more government dependency, the less workers there are to pay for it all.

In addition, fewer workers mean a smaller tax base. The smaller the tax base, the smaller the economy. The smaller the economy, the higher the unemployment rate. The higher the unemployment rate typically the higher crime rates go up as well. It becomes a vicious cycle which, as Cloward and Piven had hoped for, will eventually create a financial crisis.

Ronald Reagan once said the nine most terrifying words in the English language are "I'm from the government and I'm here to help." He also said, "The greatest social program in the world is a job." I will add my own original quote here as well, "When will the left learn that when you confiscate people's wealth it does not create more of it."[5,6]

But perhaps an even more eloquent way of putting it comes from the Iron Lady herself, the former British Prime Minister Margaret Thatcher said, "Once you give the people the idea that somehow the State can do everything better than the private individual, then you will begin to deprive human beings of one of the most essential ingredients of humanity, personal and moral responsibility."

She continues, "I place a profound belief, indeed a fervent faith, in the virtues of self-reliance and personal independence. On these virtues is found the whole case for the free society. For it is the assertion that human progress is best achieved by offering the freest possible scope, for the development of individual talents, qualified only by a respect for the qualities and the freedom of others."[7]

Since the launch of the "War on Poverty" back in 1964, the United States of America has spent an estimated $32 trillion on anti-poverty programs. With that kind of spending, we should not have even one poor person or one homeless person in the country, right? Well, I think we all can safely say that we still have plenty of poor people, and homelessness has skyrocketed in just the last few years.

According to a December 2023 study by the Department of Housing and Urban Development, more than six hundred and fifty thousand people in the United States of America experienced homelessness. This is up 12 percent from 2022, and the highest on record since 2007.[8]

You Can't Spend Your Way Out of Poverty
Let's get back to the "makers" and the "takers." You really don't have to be a mathematician to figure out that if there are too many people in the wagon, and not enough people to pull it, it's not going to go very far. That is

what universal basic income is. Class warfare is embedded in universal basic income because it breeds discontent, jealousy, and envy.

Many working Americans, also known as "the Makers," for this exercise, feel marginalized and taken advantage of knowing that their hard-earned dollars are being allocated towards programs and people who refuse to work, instead relying on the government to provide for them. These people are known as "the Takers."

So, what happens when "the Makers," the workers and taxpayers, can no longer provide free handouts for "the Takers" because they are getting taxed to death or eaten alive by historic levels of inflation? What do you think will happen when they can no longer provide benefits for those who refuse to work?

Well, it does not take a genius to figure out in a scenario like this that "the Takers" will likely riot and become violent. This is why class warfare can be so dangerous in a free society. Too many people in the wagon and not enough people to pull it creates a level of unfairness and exploitation that eventually will tear a country apart.

A Few Examples of Universal Basic Income Failures

In 2015, the country of **Finland** launched a universal basic income program in which the Finnish government doled out $658 a month to roughly two thousand unemployed families after Finland's unemployment rate reached a seventeen-year high of 10 percent.

During the years while the universal basic income program was implemented, Finland's unemployment rate remained relatively steady, dropping only about 1 percent. That was a considerable amount of money to disperse for such little in return.

In addition, according to a survey from the Social Insurance Institution, universal basic income was only supported by 35 percent of participants when it was revealed that in order to pay for the program, everybody's taxes would be raised.

Canada recently had also experimented with universal basic income to equally disastrous results. The three-year program, which lasted less than one year, gave four thousand Ontario residents $16,989 dollars per year for a single person, and $24,027 dollars per year for a couple.

The program was such a failure, that Lisa McCloud, Canada's Minister of Social Services, pulled the plug on it less than a year after it started saying, "the program is quite expensive, unsustainable, and clearly not the answer for Ontario families."

After the program had ended, Canadians were asked what they thought about the program to which 60 percent said the program made more Canadians reliant on the state and discouraged employment. Furthermore, 52 percent said universal basic income would increase taxes to unaffordable levels.

Working is inherently a human condition. It is where we fortify our pride and determination. Where we set forth and then achieve our personal goals. It is how we learn to overcome challenges and obstacles.

It is also where we learn about responsibility, teamwork, communication, and self-worth. Class warfare is embedded in welfare programs such as universal basic income through creating an environment of makers and takers.

Simply handing out money to people who have not earned it eliminates their incentive and drive to earn an income, and what should be a natural inclination towards building a successful, fulfilling, and rewarding career, instead creates a potential lifetime of poverty, dependency, and economic ruin.[9]

The great historian and Pulitzer Prize–winning Harvard Professor Oscar Handlin said this about individualism, and its importance: "Opportunity is the one prize a free society has to offer. It assures the individual has the scope within which to make the most of their abilities. It permits the community to profit from the appropriate use of talent where it is most advantageous."[10]

What Handlin meant essentially was that in America, we have equal opportunity for all, but we don't have equal results; and nor should we. This is paramount to the development of self-reliance, whereby success is achieved through hard work and not handouts.

When Americans are labeled or divided by socio-economic status, by class, or any other divisive factions, that is an example of class warfare. The 1 percent versus the 99 percent argument used by politicians and political organizations is a way to control certain people by turning them into professional victims.

Parenthetically, this same argument is also used to vilify a smaller group and shame them for their wealth and success. This troubling pattern falsely accuses successful people of somehow taking their riches from the poor, which is insane.

Have you ever seen a poor business owner or entrepreneur? Me neither, you know why? Because they worked their tail off, took risks, and gave their blood, sweat, and tears, into creating a successful business.

This is why programs like universal basic income are so detrimental. They eliminate drive, determination, and risk taking, all three are vital skill sets needed to be successful. Many politicians like to use class warfare to create victims whom they hope will turn into new voters. Using envy and pitting one class or group of people against another divides us rather than unites us.

Class Warfare and Tax Policy

Class warfare is embedded in tax policy. Change the tax policy and you can eliminate the argument. Let's examine this issue a little more closely. Is the class warfare argument valid and based on facts? Do the poor really pay more in taxes than the rich? Do wealthy Americans pay their fair share of taxes?

According to the Office of Tax Analysis, it is estimated that the top 50 percent of income earners pay close to 96 percent of all taxes. This means that the bottom 50 percent of income earners pay only 4 percent of taxes.

So, this means that close to half of Americans do not pay any taxes. Wow! Does that seem fair? Whether by design or by coincidence, what is abundantly clear is that class warfare is embedded in tax policy. So how do we fix it? The answer is quite simple; however, it will take courage and political will to get it done.

The United States Internal Revenue Service Tax Code is 6,871 pages long! That is five *War and Peace* novels! However, when you add in all the tax regulations and guideline pages, the IRS Tax Code balloons up to seventy-five thousand pages![11]

The Internal Revenue Service's Tax Code is confusing and cumbersome, and likely intentionally designed that way. The anxiety some people feel when they must file taxes is equal to the anguish one feels when they need to go to a dentist or doctor's office.

The complexity of the different forms, the confusion of which deductions are allowed, and which ones are not, and the fear of being audited once you file your returns all add to this anxiety.

How to Eliminate the Class Warfare Argument

A consumption tax, if high enough and implemented correctly, should relieve our tax burdens by eliminating or severely reducing such taxes as: income taxes, capital gains taxes, social security taxes, property taxes, estate taxes, and corporate taxes.

In this scenario, the above-mentioned taxes would all be eliminated and replaced with a 22 percent consumption-only tax on all purchased goods and services. You might be asking yourself why on earth would we want to pay a tax rate that high?

Why a 22 Percent Consumption-Only Tax?

According to Fairtax.Org, the income tax bracket most wage earners fall into is approximately 15 percent. Almost all wage earners are required to pay 7.65 percent of their income to payroll taxes. If you add the 7.65 percent to the 15 percent bracket that most wage earners fall into, that is a little more than 22 percent.

This percentage is high enough and fair enough for all taxpayers to not only keep a lot more of their money due to the elimination of all the other taxes, but more importantly, it will provide every American worker enough extra money for retirement or to reinvest back into the market thereby making the economy much stronger.

If America changed its tax policy and transitioned to a 22 percent consumption-only tax, everyone would pay the same percentage in taxes on everything they consume, not what they earn. A consumption-only tax system would not hurt the poor any more than it would help the rich. Therefore, it does not hurt the rich any more than it helps the poor.

What a consumption-only tax does is allows everyone, rich or poor, to keep a lot more of their money. In addition, by allowing wage earners to keep a lot more of their money, the effective tax rate is closer to 15 percent rather than 22 percent. This proposal also eliminates any talk of inequality, unfairness, and yes, the class warfare argument.

CHAPTER TEN

Censorship, Fake News, and How to Fix It All

Let me be abundantly clear, I am a free speech absolutist. I believe whole-heartedly that the best and most effective way to combat dangerous speech and ideas is with more speech and ideas that completely counter the narrative.

In other words, I may vehemently disagree with many people's opinions and ideas, even the dangerous ones; however, I would also fight to the death for those I passionately disagree with to be allowed to speak their minds freely about what they believe.

Censorship is a tool people use when they can't win an argument. It is designed for simple and weak-minded individuals who can't stand criticism or can't counter a narrative. So, if they disagree with something you say or believe, they immediately look for ways to silence you, rather than challenge you in a peaceful debate.

By taking this position, what these individuals are really saying is that they believe in the First Amendment right to freedom of speech so long as it is speech that they agree with. These are not free speech absolutists; these are cowards who cannot articulate their beliefs, so they shut down your ability to speak freely instead. That is not how the First Amendment works.

Former President Harry S. Truman said this about censorship: "Once a government is committed to the principles of silencing the voices of opposition, it only has one place to go, and that is down the path of increasingly repressive measures, until it becomes a source of terror to all its citizens, and creates a country where everyone lives in fear."[1]

As one of America's top ten most censored and banned voices, I know too well on a personal level what can happen when you refuse to go along with the official government narrative on a whole host of issues.

When you go from having your show or Amazon Prime and Roku Television, and on every single social media platform with millions upon millions of viewers, fans, and followers to having everything you worked for wiped out in less than forty-eight hours, it is quite difficult to come back from.[2]

But here I am, still speaking my mind, still exposing those who operate in the darkness, and still fighting to save this great country each and every day. In reality, if I'm being honest here, which of course I am, one of the secondary reasons why I decided to write this book was to break through the censorship barriers I face.

By writing this book, it gives me a way to not only teach millions of Americans how to preserve their liberties, but it also allows these bold and brave solutions to reach many more people across the country and even the world.

Besides the complete and coordinated cover-up of the coronavirus origins, which we covered in a previous chapter, there have been some atrocious examples of government colluding with Silicon Valley social media platforms to silence and censor millions of Americans.

Recent Examples of Government and Social Media Censorship

Hunter's Laptop was heavily censored, as you may remember, in the lead-up to the 2020 election. Joe Biden's son either forgot about it or just decided to leave his laptop behind in a Delaware computer repair shop. According to John Paul Mac Issac, the owner of the store, the person who left the laptop behind identified himself as Hunter Biden.

Hunter's laptop contained hundreds of thousands of emails pertaining to his father, other business associates in Ukraine, business partners from China, and elsewhere. The information contained on the laptop was quite damaging and incriminating for both Joe and Hunter Biden. It was for this reason that the information pertaining to what the FBI found on the laptop was covered up and kept from the public.

The videos, images, drug use, sexual depravity, and quite frankly, multiple crimes stored on Hunter's laptop, which I have seen, would put most people away for five hundred years or worse.

The Central Intelligence Agency, along with its former director John Brennan and many other high level intelligence officials, as well as the Federal Bureau of Investigations all knew and admitted that the laptop was indeed real.

They also knew this back in 2019, before the 2020 election, yet chose to not only cover it up completely, but coordinated their efforts with social media companies to suppress the story in order to give Joe Biden an advantage and talking point in which to attack President Trump.

You may remember the *New York Post* headline from March 2022 titled, "Spies Who Lie: 51 'Intelligence' Experts Refuse to Apologize for Discrediting True Hunter Biden Story"[3] This article by the *New York Post* names all fifty-one so-called experts who signed a fictitious letter knowing they were lying in order to interfere in the 2020 election.

It is now common knowledge throughout America and the entire world that not only was Hunter's laptop real but so was the coverup. The *New York Post* first revealed back in 2020 that the laptop from hell was real and NOT Russian disinformation.

Of course, that is when these so-called experts, including the FBI, who not only knew 100 percent that the laptop was real, but they had possession of it since 2019, decided that this information should be kept away from the general public.

What happened next goes to show that those entrusted to protect the American people instead hid vital information from them. The CIA, FBI, and others in the Intelligence Community have been weaponized against certain groups of Americans in favor of supporting others.

Have any of these intelligence officials been prosecuted? Have any of these intel officials had their security clearances stripped from them as a result of their continual prevarications? Don't hold your breath or we will have to change your name to Blue Boy because you will have turned blue before any of these remedies will have happened.

The Spies Who Cried Wolf: Fifty-One Intelligence "Experts" Who Knowingly Engaged in Election Interference and LIED about It.

1. John Brennan—former CIA director and one of the masterminds and architects behind the letter, when asked why he lied he refused to answer any questions, just simply stating, "No Comment."

2. James Clapper—former director of National Intelligence, another architect of the disinformation letter. When he was asked about why he lied, he doubled down stating, "Yes, I stand by my statement AT THE TIME and sounding such a cautionary note was appropriate." Another lie. Clapper knew when asked this question the laptop was real. However, what would one expect from someone who lied repeatedly to Congress and should have been charged with perjury?

3. Michael Hayden—another former CIA director, declined to comment or respond.

4. Leon Panetta—yet another former CIA director, declined to comment or respond.

5. Thomas Fingar—former National Intelligence Council chair, declined to comment or respond.

6. Rick Ledgett—former National Security Agency deputy director, declined to comment or respond.

7. John McLaughlin—former acting CIA director, declined to comment or respond.

8. Michael Morell—another former CIA acting director, declined to comment or respond.

9. Michael Vickers—former Defense undersecretary for intelligence, declined to comment or respond.

10. Doug Wise—former Defense Intelligence Agency deputy director, declined to comment or respond.

11. Nick Rasmussen—former National Counterterrorism Center director, declined to comment or respond.

12. Russ Travers—former National Counterterrorism Center acting director, also doubled down by saying, "We didn't know if the emails were genuine or Russian disinformation efforts." Clearly another lie

as the FBI stated the emails and the contents on Hunter's laptop were real back in 2019 when they subpoenaed and then seized the laptop from John Paul Mac-Issac.

13. John Moseman—former CIA chief of staff, declined to comment or respond.
14. Larry Pfeiffer—former CIA chief of staff, declined to comment or respond.
15. Rodney Snyder—former CIA chief of staff, declined to comment or respond.
16. Andrew Liepman—former National Counterterrorism Center deputy director, also doubled down stating, "As far as I know, I stand by my statement. No further comments as I am kind of busy right now." Wow, the arrogance!
17. Glenn Gerstell—former National Security Agency general counsel, declined to comment or respond.
18. Jeremy Bash—former CIA chief of staff, and former husband to CNN'S Dana Bash, declined to comment or respond.
19. David Priess—former CIA analyst and manager, "Thanks for reaching out. I have no further comment at this time."
20. Pam Purcilly—former CIA deputy director of analysis, declined to comment or respond.
21. Marc Polymeropoulos—former CIA senior operations officer, declined to comment or respond.
22. Chris Savos—former CIA senior operations officer, declined to comment or respond.
23. John Tullius—former CIA senior intelligence officer, declined to comment or respond.
24. David A. Vanell—former CIA senior operations officer, declined to comment or respond.
25. Kristin Wood—former CIA senior intelligence officer, declined to comment or respond.
26. David Buckley—former CIA onspector general, declined to comment or respond.
27. Nada Bakos—former CIA analyst and officer, declined to comment or respond.

28. Patricia Brandmaier—former CIA senior intelligence officer, declined to comment or respond.

29. James B. Bruce—former CIA senior intelligence officer, declined to comment or respond.

30. David Cariens—former CIA intelligence analyst, declined to comment or respond.

31. Janice Cariens—former CIA operational support officer, declined to comment or respond.

32. Paul Kolbe—former CIA senior operations officer, declined to comment or respond.

33. Peter Corsell—former CIA intelligence officer, declined to comment or respond.

34. Brett Davis—former CIA senior intelligence officer, declined to comment or respond.

35. Roger Zane George—former national intelligence officer, declined to comment or respond.

36. Steven L. Hall—former CIA senior intelligence officer, declined to comment or respond.

37. Kent Harrington—former national intelligence officer, declined to comment or respond.

38. Donald Hepburn—former national security executive, responded by saying, "I stand by my statement. I can't tell you what part is real or fake, but the thesis still stands for me, that **this was a media influence hit job.**" Wow, one intel official spoke the truth!

39. Timothy D. Kilbourn—former dean of the CIA's Kent School of Intelligence Analysis, declined to comment or respond.

40. Ronald Marks—former CIA officer, declined to comment or respond.

41. Jonna Heistand Mendez—former CIA technical operations officer, declined to comment or respond.

42. Emile Nakhlah—former CIA analyst, stated, "The whole issue was highly politicized, and I don't want to deal with it. I stand by the letter."

43. Gerald A. O'Shea—former CIA senior operations officer, declined to comment or respond.

44. Nick Shapiro—former CIA deputy chief of staff, declined to comment or respond.
45. John Sipher—former CIA senior operations officer, declined to comment or respond.
46. Stephen Slick—former National Security Council senior director, declined to comment or respond.
47. Cynthia Strand—former CIA deputy assistant director, declined to comment or respond.
48. Greg Tarbell—former CIA deputy executive director, declined to comment or respond.
49. David Terry—former national intelligence officer, declined to comment or respond.
50. Greg Treverton—former National Intelligence Council chairman, stated, "I'll pass on commenting. I haven't followed the case closely." Really? You signed the letter. So, you must have followed it a lot more closely than you will admit.
51. Winston Wiley—former CIA director of analysis, declined to comment or respond.[4]

Every single one of these people who knowingly signed this fictitious letter should not only have their security clearances revoked and their pensions stripped away, but they must be prosecuted to the fullest extent of the law. America cannot survive as a free and fair society if a large portion of the intelligence community is corrupt and working against some of the American people.

This is terrifying. These are not low-level Central Intelligence Agency, National Security Agency, or National Intelligence officers. These are individuals from some of the highest levels of the intelligence community!

Among these fifty-one officials were: four former Central Intelligence Agency directors, including two acting directors, three CIA deputy directors, five CIA chiefs of staff, and at least a dozen other CIA officers and analysts in senior positions.

In addition, you had a powerful former director of National Intelligence and five others who work right below him. Finally, six more senior members of the National Security Agency and counterterrorism experts.

All this to protect one candidate from scrutiny while interfering in an election to hurt another? Here's another question, why so many duplicate personnel? One former CIA director, chief of staff, and senior intelligence officer is not enough? Did the CIA really need to trot out fifty-one of these criminals? Why not use just seven of these corrupt officials instead?

The reason they used so many top-level directors, officers, and analysts was to try to sell their "expertise" to the media is so they could regurgitate their lies. They also trotted out these high-level officials so that no one could possibly question fifty-one of them. If there were three who wrote the letter it would not have been as impactful.

To say their influence on the outcome of the 2020 election was impactful would be an understatement. In fact, according to a report by NewsBusters. org, 17 percent of Biden voters would have not voted for him if they knew the laptop was real.

That is potentially millions of voters who likely would have changed their vote if they had access to truthful information, but of course Silicon Valley accepted their marching orders and censored anyone who posted anything about the laptop story. That is not just corruption, that is election interference.[5]

However, due to the immense and intense censorship of the story, vital information was kept from voters and as a result helped tip the election to Joe Biden's favor; that along with a whole bunch of mathematically impossible outcomes.

What these fifty-one individuals represent is the absolute worst of what Washington, DC has to offer. Political hacks, talking heads, and corrupt officials. In addition, after lying and then being proven wrong did any of them have the decency to apologize? Of course not. In fact, out of fifty-one so-called intelligence experts, forty-six out of the fifty-one refused to even comment or respond to media inquiries.

It Was Not Just the CIA—The FBI Played Its Own Part, Too

In an interview in late December 2023, Elon Musk said this about censorship on his newly purchased platform: "Almost every conspiracy theory that people had about Twitter turned out to be true. And if not, truer than people thought." What Elon Musk did was take over a problematic platform and conduct a deep audit. His findings were subsequently released to the public.

After billionaire Elon Musk bought Twitter from former CEO Jack Dorsey, he changed its name to simply "X" and began to clean house. During the cleaning process, he fired a lot of dead weight at the company and discovered a treasure trove of emails, tweets, and documents that came to be known as "The Twitter Files."

The "Twitter Files" were a series of internal documents that Twitter released in 2022 and 2023 by Matt Taibbi and various other journalists. These documents revealed exactly how the intelligence community, and in particular the Federal Bureau of Investigations colluded with Twitter to silence multiple accurate stories such as the Covid cover-ups, the vaccine injuries, and of course, the Hunter Biden laptop story.

The documents revealed how the United States government officials pressured Twitter to suppress or remove content that was not politically helpful, even though the vast majority of what they were censoring was truthful and vital information.

The Twitter Files showed that not only did our corrupt government interfere with the Hunter Biden laptop story, but the FBI was in on it too. One of the tools they used was a "back door" channel of communication in which the FBI, government officials, and the engineers and content moderators at Twitter used "shadow banning" to limit the story or flat out just removed it entirely.

How bad was the censorship? The FBI had weekly, and sometimes daily communications and meetings with Twitter officials to strategize who would be censored, which stories would be shadow banned or outright removed, and which accounts would be permanently shut down.

Twitter was the FBI, and the FBI was Twitter according to these documents. Not only was the FBI interfering with our elections, by throttling true stories, but they were also interfacing and collaborating with the Pentagon, State Department, and other governmental agencies, namely the Central Intelligence Agency, these documents reveal.

An email from Stacia Cardille, a Twitter legal executive, and James Baker, the disgraced former FBI counsel, whose image was forever tarnished in the lies about Russiagate, and an unnamed CIA operative all were communicating together to silence and ban certain voices on the platform.

This is just one of hundreds of examples of blatant collusion and coordination with the FBI and CIA and Twitter. The email reads, "Sunlight Conference tomorrow. No need for you to attend. Carnegie is doing heavy lifting. I offered to assist Nick and Yoel, but there are no academic papers to review. I was involved in the early scoping of the joint project as well. **I invited the FBI and I believe the CIA will attend too**. Please let me know if you have any further questions. Thanks, Stacia."[6]

This is what TMZ would refer to as a "smoking gun admission of guilt." The corruption, censorship, and collusion all exposed in the Twitter files shows you the depths they went to silence those they disagreed with.

In the lead-up to the 2020 election, the FBI was aggressively pushing Twitter executives to remove certain accounts that dared to post truthful information. Moreover, FBI zealots were tracking hundreds of accounts, even putting together spreadsheets with names on them to be censored or removed.

Eventually the media, or as I like to call them on my show, presstitutes, had to admit the truth. After spending years calling anyone who said that the Hunter Biden laptop story was real, liars, conspiracy theorists, and labeling it as mis- or disinformation, they were forced to finally admit the truth.[7]

My account was shadow banned for over three years on Twitter, and right before the 2020 election, I was speaking way too much truth for the FBI, CIA, and Twitter to handle, so they permanently banned me from the platform, which of course I wear as a badge of honor.

It Gets Much Worse

According to the Twitter File documents, the FBI was also on what appears to be a fishing expedition to either find or make up a connection to Russia in order to lie and justify their despicable actions.

One email says, "Hi, [redacted] after I received the accounts, **I could not find any links to Russia.** I even checked other phone linked accounts with [redacted] and could not find any indicators of a Russian proxy. **I can brainstorm with [redacted] and dig a little deeper to try to find a connection.**"[8]

The FBI's Cash for Lies Program

In addition to interfering with our elections, crushing our First Amendment rights, and targeting individuals our government does not like, the FBI was paying, or reimbursing social media platforms that censored or removed content the FBI did not like.

A shady division of the FBI known as SCALE, which stands for Safety, Content, and Law Enforcement, was a gestapo-styled division of the FBI that took delight in not protecting Americans individual rights but instead destroying them.

It is important to also note that on a guest appearance of the *Joe Rogan Show*, Facebook/Meta founder Mark Zuckerberg admitted that the FBI pressured him to remove truthful information, some of which could have saved countless lives. The FBI also pressured Facebook to ban certain stories or individuals from his platform, including the Hunter Biden laptop story.[9,10]

But it wasn't just Twitter and Facebook. Most of the media suppressed stories on the Hunter Biden laptop story as well. They also labeled anyone, including doctors, scientists, and virologists, as vaccine deniers if they showed the scientific effectiveness of ivermectin and hydroxychloroquine.

Anyone who talked negatively about lockdowns or masks was labeled a conspiracy theorist. They even censored their own studies from the Centers for Disease Control and Prevention on vaccine deaths and injuries!

Prominent and well-respected medical professionals and doctors were also on the receiving end of censorship and removal as well. Dr. Robert Malone, the inventor of mRNA technology, someone I know and had on my show, was banned for promoting accurate studies.

One of the world's most published and esteemed cardiologists, Dr. Peter McCullough, was also banned for pointing out the health risks in relation to the vaccines. These were established and well-respected doctors who were being treated like this.

Dr. Martin Kulldorff, a renowned Harvard Medical School epidemiologist, was banned for saying the vaccines were not necessary for certain groups of people. Dr. Pierre Kory, who I have interviewed and who wrote a blurb for this book, was banned for proving the effectiveness of ivermectin in early treatments, and the list goes on and on.

They called truthful factual documented proof misinformation. The only misinformation that was occurring was from these elitist, corrupt intelligence officials in the FBI and CIA, as well as government agencies, media organizations, and social media platforms.

What a sad, disgraceful, bunch of corrupt liars the majority of our intelligence community has turned into. No longer can the Federal Bureau of Investigation live up to their motto of, "Fidelity, Bravery, and Integrity."

When the FBI was actively stripping away Americans' First Amendment rights, banning individuals for their political speech, and suppressing information that could have saved countless lives in order to tip an election, I wonder if that is the "fidelity, bravery, and integrity" the FBI was referring to?

The Central Intelligence Agency is not any better. Their unofficial motto is, "And ye shall know the truth, and the truth shall make you free." Did they live up to the "truth" when they were sabotaging and interfering in our elections? Were they being "truthful" when fifty-one of their own knowingly lied about something they knew was real to cover up a story that would have hurt their preferred candidate?

Was the truth setting the CIA free when they concocted the term "conspiracy theory" to label anyone who dared to have an opposing view of the Warren Commission's official narrative?

This is why the intelligence community can no longer be trusted and should be defunded and disbanded. Once these bad actors are removed, prosecuted, and hopefully jailed for their insidious actions, only then can these agencies be rebuilt.

You know things are bad in our country when a large percentage of top-level intelligence officers knowingly sign a false letter with the goal of interfering in our elections. Then, once they get caught, instead of apologizing, they double down on their lies, and in turn target those who were brave enough to expose them. With intel officials like these who needs enemies?

Update on the 51 Frauds
On July 7, 2024, while in the final stages of editing this book, NY representative Claudia Tenney called for the prosecution of all fifty-one so called intel agents to be prosecuted under 18 U.S.C 1001, which is knowingly making false statements as a government official.

Code 1001 states, anyone "within the jurisdiction of the executive, legislative, or judicial branch of the government of the United States who falsifies, conceals, or covers up by trick, scheme, or device of material fact or makes or uses any false writing or document knowing the same to contain any materially false, fictitious, or fraudulent statement or representation is guilty and could face fines or up to five years in prison."[11]

Let's hope these fifty-one criminals get what they deserve, which is to be arrested, indicted, convicted, and sent to prison where they can write more false statements about how they did nothing wrong. These are the worst that Washington, DC has to offer and they need to held responsible for their actions.

The Fourth Estate

In order for any free society to survive it must have a free and honest press. Unfortunately, these days truthful, honest, ethical, and factual journalism is in very short supply. Love him or hate him, one of the greatest accomplishments former President Trump ever achieved was making a large percentage of Americans question what is being reported on the news as factual.

From networks like ABC, CBS, NBC, MSNBC, CNN, and even Fox News, so much of what is being reported as factual is not accurate. These networks have an agenda, and that agenda is to support narratives that fit their ideology.

So many articles being reported are inaccurate, vague, misleading, missing important context, agenda driven, narrative spun, or as former President Trump summed it up, simply "Fake News." This term was born under President Trump, and it will survive long after he is gone. We can all thank him for not only questioning the narrative but also for exposing the bias.

There are literally hundreds, maybe thousands of examples in just the last ten to twenty years alone of inaccurate reporting. I could, like the Covid chapter and the China chapter, write an entire book dedicated solely to this subject alone. However, as with those two chapters, I will give a few examples to build my case and then offer sound and solid solutions to fix the problem.

Trust in the media is at an all-time low and for very good reason. The American people have been lied to, misled, and told numerous false narratives. According to a February 2023 joint study by Gallup and the Knight Foundation, nearly three quarters of Americans said they do not trust the media. Not 25 percent, or even 30 percent, but close to 75 percent!

In the survey, they asked 5,593 adults their thoughts on the accuracy of the media and only 26 percent had a positive view of the people and organizations who report the news. In fact, half of the respondents in the survey said they disagreed with the statement that most national news organizations do not intend to mislead, misinform, or persuade the public.

Moreover, the study also revealed that only 23 percent of respondents thought that the news organizations genuinely cared about the wellbeing of their readers, viewers, and listeners. The study also found that a growing number of self-described independents, 64 percent, now hold unfavorable views towards the media.[12]

Investigative journalist Carl Bernstein, (no relation) said it best, "the lowest form of popular culture—a lack of information, misinformation, disinformation, and a contempt for the truth, has overrun real journalism."[13]

This is not only a sad situation, but it is a dangerous one as well. "A country that does not possess a free and independent press, or a press that is believable, will descend into chaos, lies, and propaganda, making it easier for the people to be controlled and the narratives made official." —Josh Bernstein. (I just came up with this one now.)

Former President Donald Trump was not only president of the United States for four years but has been the constant target of the media's disinformation campaign against him. Since the former president left office, the attacks against him have only intensified.

In order to show the fake news in action, their deceptive tactics in relation to selective editing, and their propensity to leave out important missing context, one only needs to look at these few examples to see their work in action. Sadly, most if not all, of these example's center around the former president's first term in office and a few after his term had ended.

Ten Examples of Fake News

1. In December 2017, ABC News correspondent Brian Ross aired an erroneous report that former National Security Advisor Michael

Flynn was prepared to testify that candidate Donald Trump at the time had directed him to meet with Russian officials during the campaign. *ABC News issued a retraction and Mr. Ross was suspended for four weeks then reassigned.*

2. In a perfect display of the media's propensity for shoddy journalism, also in 2017, the *New York Times,* and several other news outlets, collectively reported that all seventeen intelligence agencies had concluded that Russia interfered in the 2016 Election. *The* New York Times *was forced to issue a correction.*

3. In November 2017, CNN published an edited video that appeared to show President Trump carelessly overfeeding Koi fish on a trip to meet the late prime minister of Japan, Shinzo Abe. Abe sprinkled some food in the pond followed by dumping the rest of the box. Trump followed the exact same pattern as the prime minister, however CNN only showed President Trump dumping the box into the pond, making it look like he was overfeeding the fish. *To this day CNN never issued a retraction or removed the video.*

4. In July 2017, CNN published a report that White House communications director Anthony Scaramucci was under investigation for having ties to Kirill Dmitriev, the head of a ten-billion-dollar Russian investment fund. *The fake story led to three CNN journalists resigning and CNN issuing an apology to Scaramucci and removing the story from its website.*

5. Also in July 2017, *Newsweek* (which has written articles attacking me on multiple occasions) selectively edited a video showing the Polish First Lady Agata Kornhauser-Duda allegedly refusing to shake then President Trump's hand. In reality, the Polish First Lady decided to shake former First Lady Melania Trump's hand first. Immediately after shaking Melania's hand, the Polish First Lady then shook the hand of President Trump. Even Polish President Andrzej Duda called the initial report, "fake news." *After the full unedited version of the encounter was released, multiple news organizations, who ran the initial doctored video issued corrections, including* Newsweek.

6. In May 2017, CNN reported that former FBI director James Comey would testify that President Trump was under investigation, even

though President Trump publicly stated on three separate occasions that Comey told him he was not under investigation. During Comey's testimony to Congress, he testified that President Trump was not under investigation. *CNN issued a correction after Comey's testimony shortly afterwards.*

7. On August 15, 2017, after the conclusion of a Charlottesville, Virginia rally, President Trump was accused by literally all of the media of somehow supporting white supremacists. However, once again, his comments at his press conference were taken out of context. Here is **exactly** what President Trump said, "You had some very bad people in that group. But you also had some very fine people on both sides. You had people in that group that were there to protest the taking down of a very important statue, and the renaming of a park from Robert E. Lee to another name. *I'm not talking about the neo-Nazis and white nationalists, because they should be condemned totally.*"[14]

8. Nick Sandmann was a Covington Catholic high school student from Kentucky in Washington, DC for a March for Life Rally in January 2019. During the rally, he was confronted by a Native American man named Nathan Phillips, who himself was in town to attend an Indigenous People's March. The video showed Sandmann, smiling and wearing a red MAGA hat while Phillips was beating a drum and singing close to his face. CNN then tried to depict Sandmann as the aggressor when he clearly was not. A group called the Black Hebrew Israelites had provoked the confrontation by singing racial slurs at Sandmann and his fellow students. *CNN settled a lawsuit by Nick Sandmann one year later in January 2020 for $250 million.*[15]

9. In November 2023, Deadspin published an article written by Carron J. Phillips depicting a nine-year-old Kansas City Chiefs fan Holden Armenta as a racist because his face was painted black, and he was wearing a Native American headdress. Phillips captured a photo of the boy from just the side of his face that was painted black, ignoring the other side of his face which was painted red for the colors of the Kansas City Chiefs football team. Armenta, who is part of the Chumash tribe, was wearing the headdress to support

his team and his Native American heritage. Holden's parents filed a defamation lawsuit against Deadspin, however, at the time of this writing, it has not yet been settled. *Deadspin was sold to European company Lineup Publishing and none of the former editorial staff from Deadspin were retained, including Carron J. Phillips.*

10. Perhaps one of the biggest lies in media history was that former President Donald Trump called for violence on January 6, 2021. During his speech, he said these **exact** words, *"I know that everyone here will soon be marching over to the Capitol building to peacefully and patriotically make your voices heard."* [16]

So now that we have clearly established the fact that many of our so-called purveyors of truth, news organizations, newspapers, online publications, editors, and journalists write stories and articles that mislead, disinform, leave out context, selectively edit, or flat-out lie, what can we do to stop this type of behavior?

How do we hold those accountable who are no longer accountable to themselves? How can we make sure that those responsible for reporting the news do so in an honest and ethical manner? What should the penalties be when news organizations and journalists repeatedly report information that is blatantly false?

I think we can all understand that people can make honest mistakes from time to time. Nobody is perfect. However, in an important profession such as journalism, with lots of influence and persuasion, perfection and accuracy should be the number one focus and goal. Part of the reason we are seeing so many inaccurate stories is due to a lack of accountability, responsibility, and consequences.

Most news organizations and journalists, aside from a few lawsuits here and there, do not have to face any real consequences for writing inaccurate articles and stories. In fact, in many cases, they don't even bother to issue corrections or retractions! They just go about their business and hope nobody catches them.

The Big Lie, which was written in the 1925 book *Mein Kampf* by Adolph Hitler and is often also attributed to Hitler's minister of propaganda Joseph Goebbels states, "If you tell a lie big enough and keep repeating it, people will eventually come to believe it. The lie can be maintained only for such a time as the State can shield the people from the political, economic, and/or military consequences of the lie. It thus becomes vitally important for the State to use all its powers to repress dissent, for the truth is the mortal enemy of the lie, and thus by extension, the truth is the greatest enemy of the State."[17]

Sounds like CNN, MSNBC, ABC, CBS, NBC, the *New York Times*, the *Washington Post, Newsweek, USA Today,* and many other news organizations and journalists are practicing the Big Lie, hoping the people will eventually believe it.

One can only surmise that based on these revelations, there seems to be a concerted effort by most of the media to mislead the American people. Sadly, most of the American media is trying to convey a certain type of message to the American people even if that message is inaccurate.

Since President Trump took office and the years after his presidency ended, more and more Americans are waking up to the fact that maybe the former president was right all along when he accurately labeled the majority of the American media as "Fake News."

We Need a Truth in Media Act

I have never been a fan of trying to legislate our way out of a problem; however, if we are going to hold the media accountable, it unfortunately will be necessary. One inaccurate story could be seen as just an honest mistake. Two inaccurate stories could be seen as shoddy journalism. Three inaccurate stories or more from one journalist or media company, however, is a purposeful agenda.

In order to hold our media figures, journalists, and news organizations on both sides of the political spectrum and down the middle accountable for what they report, there must be universally recognized and accepted accuracy standards and consequences. So, what then should the consequences be for writing inaccurate or misleading stories?

I think that should depend on the frequency and severity of the infractions. For companies like CNN and the *New York Times*, who repeatedly run false stories, there should be fines, suspensions, and even permanent restrictions of broadcasting licenses.

For journalists who work for the news organizations, or even independently, there should be heavy fines depending on the frequency and severity of these infractions, even up to a permanent ban to practice journalism. **Journalism is not a right; it is a privilege, and it must be practiced with ethics, truthfulness, and responsibility.**

In addition, every journalist, whether independent like myself or employed by an organization, should be licensed to practice journalism. If news organizations and journalists had real accountability and consequences, fake news would soon be a thing of the past.

You need a contractor's license to build houses. You need a teaching certificate to be a teacher. You need a law license to be an attorney. But you don't need a license to report the news? One of the most impactful jobs one could have?

Our media companies and media figures have an awesome responsibility to report only facts and not fiction. They must be honest and ethical, without a political agenda. The only agenda any member of the media should ever have is towards the truth.

In addition, as stated previously, Congress must act immediately and repeal Section 230 of the Communications Decency Act. This move will force tech companies to choose to be a publisher or a platform. It will also allow individuals and organizations who have been shadow banned, censored, or banned outright from different social media platforms the right to sue these companies for violating their First Amendment right to free speech.

Finally, as a part of this proposed legislation, there also needs to be a permanent ban on all political parties, politicians, lobbyists, activist groups, intelligence personnel, and government officials from colluding with, or exerting pressure on any social media companies to censor the views and opinions of certain groups and individuals they do not agree with.

If these changes are implemented, every American, no matter their political persuasion, will be able to voice their opinion and participate in healthy debate. This is what is supposed to separate America from many countries of the world.

CONCLUSION

Preserving Liberty

Well, it looks as though we have come to the end of our journey together. I hope you have learned a lot of information you never knew before. I hope that you liked my easy flow writing style, my sarcasm, and of course my occasional attempts to humor you.

I hope you have had many sudden and audible gasps—the kind that makes someone right next to you ask, "what's wrong?" I hope you have read multiple details in this book that were so shocking that you had to grab your glasses and read them again. Most of all, I hope you have learned that, although our journey together is ending, the fight to preserve our liberties is just beginning.

Yes, you. I'm talking directly to you, I pray that you become civically active and engaged. I pray that you take what I have laid out here in this book and share it with many other people. I pray that you are motivated and ready to act upon these ideas and help take them from concept to reality.

All change happens at the local level. However, it's not just in your town, in your local community, in your neighborhood, or even on your own block. Change starts within every one of us by refusing to abide by or accept the status quo.

Be the change you want to see. Run for city council. Run for your local board of supervisors. Run for precinct committee member. Run for your state legislature. Work at your local county recorder's office. Do door knocking, canvassing, and phone banking.

Start petitions and get them on your state ballot. Start networking groups so you can teach others the importance of civic engagement. Volunteer to be a poll watcher. Keep an eye on the parking lots. If you see something strange, report it.

America won't survive with more ballots under tables, fictitious water leaks, and after midnight backdoor deliveries. We need to have eyes everywhere. Create teams and shifts so some can watch the polling stations, some can watch the drop boxes, and some can watch the counting centers.

This country was founded by patriots who fought what seemed insurmountable odds to victory and independence. When we all work together there is nothing we can't accomplish, including preserving our liberties.

The American people truly have all the power, they just don't realize it, or know how to use it. Hopefully, this book can be used as an effective tool to help discover their power. The American people, not the government, are in control of this country. It is about time we started acting like it.

Writing a book is like sitting in the front seat of a roller coaster with all the readers behind you. Everybody is strapped in tight and ready for the experience. Some are anxious, some are excited, and some are terrified, including at times, even myself.

On this journey together, we went through some dark and scary areas but eventually came out into the light. We went from steep descents to rapid ascents, and a lot of twists and turns. Some of it was bumpy. Some of it was smooth. All of it was a learning experience.

I have learned so much about myself by writing this book. This experience has taught me that when given the opportunity of a lifetime you seize it. I learned not to be afraid of the experience and instead fully embrace it. I learned that now my words and ideas will forever be recorded in history and will live on long after I am gone in the hearts and minds of others.

Good ideas cannot become great ideas until they are acted upon. America was born on an idea as these famous words from Thomas Jefferson remind us: "We hold these truths to be self-evident, that all men are created equal, that they are endowed by their Creator with certain unalienable Rights, that among these are Life, Liberty and the pursuit of Happiness."

Most people think this section of the preamble is the most significant. As I have shown throughout the writing of this book, I don't think like everybody else. In my opinion, this part of our great Declaration of Independence is just as important, if not **more**:

"That to secure these rights, Governments are instituted among Men, deriving their just powers from the consent of the governed. That whenever any Form of Government becomes destructive of these ends, **it is the Right of the People to alter or abolish it**, and to institute a new Government, laying its foundation on such principles and organizing its powers in such form, as to them shall seem most likely to affect their Safety and Happiness."

"There are but two potential violators of man's rights: the criminals and the government. The great achievement of the United States was to draw a distinction between these two by forbidding to the second the legalized version of the activities of the first." —Ayn Rand, 1963 "Man's Rights."

For those of you who are familiar with my show, I will end this book the same way I end every broadcast I have ever recorded in my career.

"Those are my thoughts, what are yours?"

Preserving Liberty . . .

Notes

Introduction

1 Ronald Reagan's inaugural address, January 20, 1981, www.presidency.ucsb.edu/documents/inaugural-address-11.
2 https://uwsboard.com/viewtopic.php?t=32414.
3 www.goodreads.com/quotes/13915-freedom-is-never-more-than-one-generation-away-from-extinction.

Chapter One

1 www.finder.com/personal-loans/doomsday-prepper-statistics.
2 www.heritage.org/voterfraud.
3 https://bipartisanpolicy.org/blog/four-things-to-know-about-noncitizen-voting/.
4 www.fairus.org/issue/noncitizens-voting-violations-and-us-elections.
5 www.judicialwatch.org/illegal-immigrants-drivers-licenses/.
6 https://finance.yahoo.com/news/heartland-rasmussen-poll-one-five-161100197.html.
7 www.census.gov/newsroom/press-releases/2021/2020-presidential-election-voting-and-registration-tables-now-available.html
8 https://ballotpedia.org/Ballot_harvesting_laws_by_state.
9 www.nbcnews.com/politics/elections/online-vulnerable-experts-find-nearly-three-dozen-u-s-voting-n1112436.
10 www.wlns.com/news/michigan/windows-in-counting-room-at-detroit-tcf-center-being-covered/.
11 https://constitution.congress.gov/browse/essay/artI-S4-C1-2/ALDE_00013577/.
12 https://time.com/5936036/secret-2020-election-campaign/.
13 Ibid.
14 https://capitalresearch.org/article/states-banning-zuck-bucks/.
15 https://publicintegrity.org/politics/elections/who-counts/election-partnership-voters-consequences-eric/.
16 www.yahoo.com/news/map-29-million-americans-live-153000154.html.

Chapter Two

1 https://x.com/Real_RobN/status/1790185258949984509/photo/1.
2 https://therecord.media/sentinelone-to-acquire-krebs-stamos-group.
3 https://omaha.com/news/local/government-politics/photos-charlie-kirk-hosts-rally
   -for-nebraska-to-become-a-winner-take-all-electoral-state/collection_75ecde64-f6e
   1-11ee-89e7-23317d195773.html#1.
4 www.jetpunk.com/user-quizzes/176412/all-3142-counties-of-the-united-states-on
   -a-map.
5 www.businessinsider.com/half-of-the-united-states-lives-in-these-counties-2013-9.
6 www.cdc.gov/nchs/hus/sources-definitions/msa.htm.
7 https://apnews.com/article/archive-fact-checking-5265150031.
8 www.factcheck.org/2023/08/number-of-counties-won-in-presidential-election
   -doesnt-determine-outcome/.
9 www.azquotes.com/author/86531-Josh_Bernstein#google_vignette.

Chapter Three

1 http://libertytree.ca/quotes/Joseph.Story.Quote.78FB.
2 https://lawyerfrommexico.com/mexico-immigration-laws-penalties/.
3 https://usafacts.org/articles/what-can-the-data-tell-us-about-unauthorized
   -immigration/.
4 www.fairus.org/legislation/executive/2023-marks-highest-level-illegal-immigration
   -us-history.
5 www.cnn.com/2023/09/13/health/overdose-deaths-record-april-2023/index.html.
6 https://cis.org/Report/ForeignBorn-Share-and-Number-Record-Highs-February
   -2024.
7 www.speaker.gov/64-times-the-biden-administration-intentionally-undermined
   -border-security/.
8 www.thenewhumanitarian.org/maps-and-graphics/2024/01/15/Darién
   -gap-migration-crisis-six-graphs-and-one-map.
9 https://homeland.house.gov/2024/04/30/new-documents-reveal-airports-used-by
   -secretary-mayorkas-to-fly-hundreds-of-thousands-of-inadmissible-aliens-into-u-s
   -via-chnv-mass-parole-scheme/.
10 www.cbp.gov/newsroom/national-media-release/cbp-releases-march-2024
   -monthly-update.
11 https://nypost.com/2024/05/16/us-news/illegal-crossings-at-us-canada-border-on
   -pace-to-shatter-record/.
12 www.fairus.org/blog/2024/04/01/northern-border-sees-114-increase-illegal-alien
   -encounters-first-four-months-fy.

Chapter Four

1 www.usatoday.com/story/news/politics/onpolitics/2017/08/04/here-12-major
   -leaks-donald-trump-era/539674001/.

2   https://thehill.com/blogs/congress-blog/the-administration/151168-president
    -obama-loves-leaks-despises-whistleblowers/.
3   https://thehill.com/homenews/4340803-the-hills-top-lobbyists-2023/.
4   https://ballotpedia.org/118th_Congress_legislative_calendar.
5   www.pcmag.com/news/5-modern-technologies-the-jetsons-accurately-predicted
    -60-years-ago.
6   www.forbes.com/advisor/business/remote-work-statistics/.
7   https://www.politico.com/story/2013/01/poll-75-percent-want-hill-term
    -limits-086378.
8   https://en.wikipedia.org/wiki/United_States_Foreign_Intelligence_Surveillance
    _Court.

Chapter Five

1   https://home.treasury.gov/policy-issues/financial-markets-financial-institutions
    -and-fiscal-service/debt-limit.
2   www.cnbc.com/2024/03/01/the-us-national-debt-is-rising-by-1-trillion-about-every
    -100-days.html.
3   www.cagw.org/reporting/pig-book.
4   www.co.dakota.mn.us/News/Pages/turtle-tunnels.aspx.
5   www.politico.com/magazine/story/2014/02/government-spending-tom-coburn
    -103189/.
6   www.investopedia.com/financial-edge/0410/6-outrageous-political-earmarks.aspx.
7   https://dailycitizen.focusonthefamily.com/1-5-million-to-walk-lizards-on-treadmills
    -ten-crazy-things-uncle-sam-spent-your-money-on-this-year/.
8   www.azquotes.com/quote/825925.
9   https://millennialmoney.com/statistics-about-millionaires/#demographics.
10 www.taxpolicycenter.org/taxvox/4-trillion-us-wealth-stashed-overseas-much-it-tax
    -havens.
11 www.thebalancemoney.com/national-debt-by-year-compared-to-gdp-and-major
    -events-3306287.

Chapter Six

1   https://worldpopulationreview.com/country-rankings/gun-ownership-by-country.
2   www.amazon.com/Hitlers-Table-Talk-1941-1944-Conversations/dp/1929631057.
3   https://en.wikipedia.org/wiki/Joseph_Stalin#In_Lenin's_government.
4   https://en.wikipedia.org/wiki/Great_Leap_Forward.
5   https://en.wikipedia.org/wiki/Cultural_Revolution.
6   https://en.wikipedia.org/wiki/Mao_Zedong.
7   www.atf.gov/rules-and-regulations/national-firearms-act.
8   https://en.wikipedia.org/wiki/Federal_Firearms_Act_of_1938.
9   https://en.wikipedia.org/wiki/Firearms_Control_Regulations_Act_of_1975.
10 https://crimeresearch.org/2022/05/breaking-down-mass-public-shooting-data
    -from-1998-through-may-2022-info-on-weapons-used-gun-free-zones-racial-age
    -and-gender-demographics/.

11 www.ojp.gov/ncjrs/virtual-library/abstracts/gun-free-school-zones-act-1990.

12 www.security.org/blog/a-timeline-of-school-shootings-since-columbine/.

13 www.axios.com/2017/12/15/deadliest-mass-shootings-modern-us-history.

14 https://en.wikipedia.org/wiki/District_of_Columbia_v._Heller.

15 www.law.cornell.edu/uscode/text/32/109.

16 www.armfor.uscourts.gov/ConfHandout/2023ConfHandout/Leider6Militia Clause2Organization.pdf.

17 https://en.wikipedia.org/wiki/State_defense_force.

18 www.concealedcarry.com/gun-quotes-from-our-founding-fathers-2nd-amendment/.

Chapter Seven

1   https://en.wikipedia.org/wiki/Conspiracy_theory.

2   https://centerforhealthsecurity.org/our-work/tabletop-exercises/event-201 -pandemic-tabletop-exercise#players.

3   https://en.wikipedia.org/wiki/Johns_Hopkins_Center_for_Health_Security.

4   https://www.weforum.org/

5   https://capitalresearch.org/article/they-really-believe-youll-be-happy/.

6   www.gatesfoundation.org/.

7   www.vox.com/recode/22528659/bill-gates-largest-farmland-owner-cascade-investments.

8   https://centerforhealthsecurity.org/our-work/tabletop-exercises/event-201 -pandemic-tabletop-exercise#players.

9   www.scribd.com/document/496518155/Email-Exchanges-Between-the-National -Academy-of-Science-and-the-Scientists#from_embed.

10 https://usrtk.org/wp-content/uploads/2020/12/NASEM_Andersen-Email _Baric-1.pdf.

11 https://en.chinacdc.cn/about/academicians/202201/t20220105_255656.html.

12 www.washingtontimes.com/news/2020/jan/26/coronavirus-link-to-china -biowarfare-program-possi/.

13 www.nature.com/articles/nm.3985.

14 www.science.org/do/10.1126/article.71505/full/_43088final-1710959188277.pdf.

15 www.vanityfair.com/news/2023/11/covid-origins-warnings-nih-department-of-energy.

16 https://theintercept.com/2021/09/23/coronavirus-research-grant-darpa/.

17 https://oversight.house.gov/wp-content/uploads/2024/05/Tab-2-EHA-SUSP4D -ARM_05.15.2024_signed.pdf.

18 https://oversight.house.gov/wp-content/uploads/2022/02/Letter-to-Dr-Andersen .pdf.

19 https://oversight.house.gov/wp-content/uploads/2023/06/2023.06.29-BRW-Letter -to-DM-Re.-Origins_Redacted_Final.pdf.

20 https://twitter.com/LPMisesCaucus/status/1630895706465611777/photo/1.

21 https://nypost.com/2024/05/16/opinion/we-now-know-the-likely-truth-about -covid-and-how-scientists-lied/.

22 https://oversight.house.gov/release/covid-select-subcommittee-releases-dr-faucis -transcript-highlights-key-takeaways-in-new-memo/.

23 https://theconversation.com/face-masks-affect-how-children-understand-speech-differently-from-adults-new-research-185979.
24 https://blog.whitecoatwaste.org/2021/10/05/wcw-investigation-fauci-wasted-1m-to-de-bark-poison- beagle-puppies/.
25 www.ncbi.nlm.nih.gov/pmc/articles/PMC4857470/.
26 https://blog.whitecoatwaste.org/2021/07/30/fauci-funding-wasteful-deadly-dog-tests/.
27 https://blog.whitecoatwaste.org/2019/10/30/video-tax-dollars-wasted-to-cripple-monkeys-with-toxic-brain-injections/.
28 https://iccinvestigation.wordpress.com/.
29 www.documentcloud.org/documents/20793561-leopold-nih-foia-anthony-fauci-emails#document/p153.
30 https://sph.unc.edu/sph-news/remdesivir-developed-at-unc-chapel-hill-proves-effective-against-covid-19-in-niaid-human-clinical-trials/.
31 www.newsweek.com/fauci-making-millions-during-covid-pandemic-sparks-backlash-1828484.
32 https://oversight.house.gov/release/covid-select-subcommittee-releases-dr-faucis-transcript-highlights-key-takeaways-in-new-memo/.

Chapter Eight

1 www.goodreads.com/quotes/17973-victorious-warriors-win-first-and-then-go-to-war-while.
2 www.brainyquote.com/quotes/sun_tzu_384831.
3 www.cnn.com/2023/12/19/business/american-companies-foreign-owners-us-steel/index.html.
4 www.sunmark.org/connect/sunmark-360/all-american-brands-are-actually-made-china-and-other-countries.
5 https://positivechangepc.com/uncategorized/american-companies-that-are-no-longer-american/.
6 www.goodreads.com/quotes/358692-there-is-no-instance-of-a-nation-benefitting-from-prolonged.
7 www.thesun.co.uk/news/10925668/coronavirus-patients-welded-homes-china/
8 www.dailymail.co.uk/news/article-11597955/Chinese-families-start-burning-bodies-loved-ones-streets-amid-Covid-explosion.html
9 https://www.cfr.org/backgrounder/chinas-massive-belt-and-road-initiative
10 www.nbcnews.com/politics/national-security/china-spy-balloon-collected-intelligence-us-military-bases-rcna77155.
11 https://learningenglish.voanews.com/a/walmart-shifts-to-india-cuts-china-imports/7377475.html.
12 https://importdojo.com/made-in-prc/.
13 https://counterhate.com/research/deadly-by-design/.
14 https://en.wikipedia.org/wiki/Zhang_Yiming.
15 https://www.forbes.com/sites/alexandralevine/2023/05/30/tiktok-creators-data-security-china/?sh=6a95f7f17048.

16 https://en.wikipedia.org/wiki/Temu_(marketplace.
17 https://en.wikipedia.org/wiki/Pinduoduo.
18 https://www.dol.gov/agencies/ilab/against-their-will-the-situation-in-xinjiang.
19 www.bloomberg.com/news/articles/2023-06-13/temu-sells-products-in-us-linked
    -to-forced-labor-in-china-s-uyghur-region?embedded-checkout=true.
20 https://thefederalnewswire.com/stories/653890172-new-report-finds-shein-temu
    -fueled-by-slave-labor-in-xinjiang.
21 www.bbc.com/news/business-67752413.
22 www.nytimes.com/2023/06/22/business/economy/shein-temu-forced-labor-china
    .html.
23 www.rubio.senate.gov/rubio-merkley-uyghur-forced-labor-prevention-act
    -becomes-law/.
24 https://finance.yahoo.com/news/chinas-temu-takes-over-17-204905173.html.
25 www.brainyquote.com/quotes/sun_tzu_398639.

Chapter Nine
1 https://www.azquotes.com/author/86531-Josh_Bernstein.
2 https://en.wikipedia.org/wiki/Cloward%E2%80%93Piven_strategy.
3 https://moneyzine.com/personal-finance-resources/how-many-people-are
    -on-welfare/.
4 https://www.monticello.org/research-education/thomas-jefferson-encyclopedia
    /government-big-enough-give-you-everything-you-wantspurious-quotation/.
5 https://www.brainyquote.com/quotes/ronald_reagan_128358.
6 https://www.azquotes.com/author/86531-Josh_Bernstein.
7 https://fee.org/articles/margaret-thatcher-on-socialism-20-of-her-best-quotes/.
8 www.cbsnews.com/news/homeless-record-america-12-percent-jump-high-rents/.
9 https://www.newsweek.com/universal-basic-income-moral-hazard-opinion
    -1863775.
10 https://en.wikipedia.org/wiki/Oscar_Handlin.
11 https://equifund.com/blog/tax-liability-meaning/.

Chapter Ten
1 https://www.goodreads.com/quotes/17832-once-a-government-is-committed-to
    -the-principle-of-silencing.
2 https://conservativefiringline.com/conservative-talker-josh-bernstein-pays-price
    -for-telling-truth-in-2020-more-big-tech-censorship/.
3 https://nypost.com/2022/03/18/intelligence-experts-refuse-to-apologize-for
    -smearing-hunter-biden-story/.
4 https://nypost.com/2022/03/18/intelligence-experts-refuse-to-apologize-for
    -smearing-hunter-biden-story/.
5 https://www.newsbusters.org/blogs/nb/rich-noyes/2020/11/24/special-report
    -stealing-presidency-2020.
6 https://x.com/mtaibbi/status/1606701425803005953.

7   https://nypost.com/2022/03/30/washington-post-admits-hunter-biden-laptop-is
     -real/.
8   www.brownstoneresearch.com/bleeding-edge/what-the-twitter-files-have
     -revealed-so-far/.
9   https://thehill.com/policy/technology/3616579-zuckerberg-tells-rogan-that-facebook
     -suppressed-hunter-biden-laptop-story-after-fbi-warning-defends-agency-as
     -legitimate-institution/.
10 www.nationalreview.com/news/mark-zuckerberg-says-facebook-censored-true
     -covid-claims-at-request-of-health-establishment/.
11 www.aol.com/house-republican-calls-51-prosecuted-170405671.html.
12 www.niemanlab.org/2023/02/half-of-americans-think-most-national-news-orgs
     -intend-to-mislead-or-misinform-the-public/.
13 www.brainyquote.com/quotes/carl_bernstein_181176.
14 https://710wor.iheart.com/featured/mark-simone/content/2019-10-09-a-list-of
     -some-of-the-fake-news-stories-by-the-media-against-donald-trump/.
15 www.foxnews.com/media/cnn-disinformation-examples-smollett-collusion
     -covington-rogan-media.
16 https://twitter.com/JonathanTurley/status/1550273913296490503.
17 www.jewishvirtuallibrary.org/joseph-goebbels-on-the-quot-big-lie-quot.

Acknowledgments

Professional Acknowledgments

First, I want to start out with my professional colleagues, friends, talk show hosts, and frequent guests that have appeared on my show. I will save personal relationships, family members, and those closest to me for the end. Publicly known figures and professional colleagues will be addressed by name.

As one of America's most targeted investigative journalists over the past ten-plus years, I have gained lots of supporters and an equal number of detractors. Throughout my career, I have gone after, spotlighted, unveiled, unmasked, and exposed numerous individuals, organizations, activist groups, politicians, intel officials, even judges.

As a result of these actions, I have been shadow banned, shut down, canceled, targeted, and even threatened. Therefore, for my security, my family's security, and the security of my closest friends, I will refrain from addressing any private person in my life by their names.

My very first thanks go of course to God, as nothing would be possible without him.

Of course, this book would also not be possible without the amazing people at Skyhorse Publishing who gave me this incredible opportunity to help preserve our liberties. Thank you so much!

Also, I need to give a quick shout-out to Eminem and his hit song "Lose Yourself," which my wife would play to me while we were out walking our dogs each night to keep me focused and motivated on writing this book.

Although I am not a huge rap fan, these lines from "Lose Yourself" really hit home: "You own it, you better never let it go. You only get one shot, do not miss your chance. This opportunity comes once in a lifetime." These lyrics were something that really resonated with me and kept my focus and attention on getting this book written and on time.

I will start with these three individuals, who collectively gave me incredible opportunities and helped my career tremendously. These individuals, two who sadly are no longer with us, believed in me and saw something in me that at the time I might not have seen in myself. In no particular order they are:

Dave Pratt was an important person who believed in me early on and taught me a lot about broadcasting. "The Morning Mayor" as he is known to his legion of fans, ruled the airwaves for over three decades as an award-winning radio host and DJ. Dave gave me my very first opportunity to be in a real studio, with real producers, and real engineers.

Dave taught me a lot about the broadcasting business and how to be a great host. Dave taught me voice control and inflection, he taught me rhythm and cadence, he taught me about pitch and tone, he taught me how far or near to be from the microphone, how to do rejoiners, when to be funny, when to be serious, etc. I will forever be grateful for those one-on-ones in the conference room at his studios.

Dan Weber was the late founder of the Association of Mature American Citizens, a fifty-plus senior advocacy group with two million members. Dan gave me a huge break that catapulted my career into another stratosphere.

After our interview together on my show, he asked me if I would like to be his National Spokesman, to which I immediately agreed. There I was, barely forty years old at the time and not even old enough to be a member of his group, and I am representing seniors! It was an incredible three-year run.

Barry Farber, the late great legendary radio talk show host, who is listed number nine on the top ten greatest radio talk show hosts in US history, was a huge influence on me and my mentor. In fact, even Sean Hannity was mentored by Barry, so that is some pretty good company to be associated with. Barry is also a member of the Talk Radio Hall of Fame and was on the air for sixty years!

Barry was like a second grandfather to me, and I probably appeared as a guest on his show over three hundred times. Barry spoke twenty-five languages and traveled the world as a journalist. He lived through so much history, and his stories were legendary. Every show we did together was a historical learning experience for me.

Barry would always tell me, "Kid, you're gonna take over the world." To which I would always reply, "Barry, I don't want to take over the world, I want to save it instead." When Barry was alive, he spent most of his life fighting to preserve our liberties; I am honored to take over the mantle from him.

Finally, the amazing talk radio hosts who I have had the pleasure to get to know and be a guest on their shows. With well over four thousand radio interviews conducted over my career, there is no way I can recall or remember every show I have been on, nor can I thank every host.

Instead, I will name the twenty-five hosts plus one that I got to know and had the opportunity to appear as a guest on many occasions. Every one of these hosts has afforded me the opportunity to grow my brand, and hopefully in return, I was able to educate and entertain their audiences.

Here they are in no particular order: J. D. Hayworth, Wayne Allyn Root, Rusty Humphries, Perry Atkinson, Lou Vickery, Clint Bellows, Mike Shikman, Terry Lowery, Jason Olbourne, Chuck Wilder, Mark Cox, Greg Young, Ben Rockwell, Kerry Lutz, Jim Engster, Larry Pratt, Rob Schilling, Dr. Bill Deagle, George Nemah, Tim Tapp, Paul Harrell, Jimmy Lakey, Gail Fallen, Bill Muckler, Charles Moskowitz, and Jennifer Meadows, who I thank for giving me my start in radio with the *Grit and Grace Show*.

Finally, these are my all-stars. These are the folks I know or knew personally and have been a guest on their shows too many times to count. These are people who have been with me since the very beginning.

They have been there for the best of times and the worst of times, but none of them ever abandoned me when I was being silenced, censored, and shut down. In fact, they promoted me even more when I needed that promotion the most. For that, and their loyalty, I am truly grateful.

Again, in no particular order: *Ringside Politics* with Jeff Crouere, *The Jiggy Jaguar Show*, the late Barry Farber, *PIJN News* with Gordon Klingenschmitt, *The Hub Radio Show* with Ray Michaels and Ron Ludders, *The Pete Santilli Show*, *News Talk with Duke Brooks*, *The Charles Butler Show*, *Bill Martinez Live*, and *The Allan Nathan Show*. Thank you all for helping me regain my audience!

A special great BIG thank you to all those who wrote a blurb for my book! I really appreciate your kind words and endorsement of my work! Alan Dershowitz, Congressman Paul Gosar, Roger Stone, Dr. Pierre Kory, A. J. Rice, Retired Marine Major Fred Galvin, Sheriff Mark Lamb, State Senator Anthony Kern, State Senator Wendy Rogers, State Majority Leader Sonny Borrelli, Maison Deschamps, Trevor Loudon, Jim Hoft, Edward Dowd, Ben Bergquam, James Lowe, Jason Olbourne, and Jeff Crouere.

Very special thanks to my good friend and patriot Congressman Paul Gosar for writing the foreword to this book!

Also, I have interviewed well over five hundred guests over the last ten-plus years on my show, and I am grateful for every one of them. However, I cannot name them all, so I will name some of the best interviews in no particular order:

Roger Stone, Kari Lake, Majorie Taylor Greene, Dr. Ben Carson, Alan Dershowitz, Judge Jeanine Pirro, James O' Keefe, Mike Lindell, Dr. Robert Malone, Dr. Naomi Wolf, Peter Navarro, Frank Gaffney, Allen West, Robert Kiyosaki, Dr. John Gray, Montel Williams, Dick Morris, Paul Manafort, Brandon Straka, Christina Bobb, Pamela Geller, Patrick Bryne, Ed Henry, J. Michael Waller, Fred Galvin, Jerome Corsi, Kathleen Willey, Dolly Kyle, Gregg Phillips, Larry Klayman, Wendy Rogers, Susan Swift, Alex Kendrick, Joe Newby, Garland Favorito, Sargis Sangari, Michael Cutler, Evan Sayet, Micajah Jackson, Derek Amato, the late Herbert London, the late Curtis Ellis, the late Lynette Hardaway from *Diamond and Silk*, the late attorney F. Lee Bailey, the late Admiral James "Ace" Lyons, and the late actress Cindy Williams.

Now I am going to do something most would not do. I am going to highlight a few of my political adversaries as well. Let's start by thanking every independent YouTuber who has ever taken the time to devote an entire video to attacking me. I have seen quite a few of these, and I must admit some of them are quite hilarious.

To *Newsweek, The Atlantic, USA Today*, thank you for writing hit pieces about me. To other smaller independent publications, thank you for caring enough about the things I say to write nasty articles about me.

To Cenk Uygur from the *Young Turks*, thank you for allowing me the opportunity to come on your show and destroy you in a debate. If you have the appetite for another beatdown you know where to find me.

To Dr. Rashad Richey, thank you for getting so triggered that you had to cut off my microphone during our debate together because I was kicking your ass on your own show. We should do it again sometime, except on my show where we don't believe in cutting off microphones.

How could I forget to give a BIG thank you to the now retired NBC News Correspondent Brian Williams, for taking time out of one of the final broadcasts of his career to attack me personally by name in front of the whole country. I would love some more publicity like that!

Finally, to my biggest adversary of them all, Right Wing Watch, which is an extremist group masquerading as some type of legitimate online publication. You folks have been so triggered by the things I've said over these last ten-plus years that to date you have written 368 articles or mentions about me.

Your organization is directly responsible for my constant threats and targeting. However, just remember, all publicity is good publicity, and I am immensely proud of every one of those articles, and I wear them as a badge of honor to know that over the years I have been that over the target.

I'd also like to thank every veteran—past and current military member. Let's face it, you are the ones who really are preserving our liberties. Special thanks to all my veteran friends, and to my newest, I thank you all for your service.

Last, but certainly not least and before I get into the personal side of things, there would not be a me without all of you, my devoted, loyal, and loving fans. For those of you who have stuck with me from the beginning, I thank you so much. For every single subscriber, past and present, I am so humbled and appreciative of your dedication and support!

To my special bunch of commenters, you all know who you are. No matter how busy or tired I might be at the end of each day, one of my joys is replying to your daily comments! To the Full Access Friday crowd, it has been a real joy getting to know all of you and interact with you each week on a more personal level. I really appreciate you all taking time out of each Friday night to join me!

To my interview producer and Full Access Friday administrator, I could not ask for a better person and assistant. I am truly blessed to have you as a dear friend.

To my videographer, and dear friend, who has been with me all the way back to my Facebook days. He has had some health issues, and I want you to know you are always in our prayers. I have worked with many videographers in my career, but you are by far the best and most dedicated to the cause.

Finally, my dear friend and head of my security team, you have helped me out so much and have been so generous. You have protected **jbushow. com** from so many attacks that even when one rarely gets through, no matter how bad it is, you always have us back up in hours not days. I could not do what I do daily without you.

Personal Acknowledgments

To my childhood friends, some of whom I still talk with to this day, and to my buddy who moved out of state twelve years ago, who would have ever thought that our political conversations in the late 1990s would have not only turned into this book, but also a career?

To my brother's best friend, who has always supported me and joins us live each Friday night, you're the best. To my wife's best friend, and fellow night owl, and the only person we know that is still up at three in the morning like us, thank you for your support.

To my dear friend, who has become a family member, thank you for always being there for me and my son. You have been a big part of our lives, and we are so grateful for it. Thank you for helping me when I needed it the most. I am so thankful I was able to give back when I could.

To my wife's extended family, thank you all for your love and support. I appreciate you all. Your family dynamic is something every family should strive for.

To all my extended family and cousins on my mother's side and my late father's side, I thank you all for your love and support and for always asking me, "so what is it again that you do?"

To my aunt and uncle and cousins on my father's side, thank you for always supporting me when I needed it the most. To my aunt, who is battling some health issues at the time, please know you are always in my prayers. Thank you both for supporting your great nephew and his musical ambitions and being there for him as well. I am forever grateful. I love you all.

To my aunt and uncle and cousins on my mother's side, thank you all for always being there and supporting me. To my uncle who is battling health issues right now, just know you are always in my prayers. I love you all.

To my stepdaughter, who has been a joy to get to know and watch turn into the woman she is today, you are going to do great things. I love you.

To my sister, my brother-in-law, and my nephews, thank you all for your support. To my sister, for always being there and looking after your baby brother, to this day you are the only person that can call me squirt and get away with it, lol. I love you all.

To my brother and sister-in-law, and my nephew, thank you all for your support. To my big brother, who as a kid I always looked up to, it is amazing with all the crazy stuff we did together that we made it out alive and this far, lol. I love you all.

To my late father, practical joker, and to this day still the funniest person I have ever known. I know you would be very proud of this moment for me. Thank you for teaching me to never take no for an answer and always fight for what I believe in. Your great advice is something I use every day of my life. I miss you so much. I love you.

To my mother and stepdad, so glad you both decided to join me out here. It is so great to have you both so close by and I appreciate your support. I love you both.

To my mother, thank you for always being there and for being an amazing mother, who no doubt learned how to be so exceptional from grandma and grandpa. Thank you for teaching me to never be a victim and for always standing up for myself.

Thank you for building up my self-confidence and molding me into the man I am today. Thank you for teaching me love and compassion and for always calling me your "sunshine on a cloudy day." I love you.

To my dearest son, you are so bright, so gifted, and have such a big heart. You are going to climb to heights that hopefully will far surpass that of your father's. It has been the joy of my life watching you grow up from a little boy into a man. I am so proud of you.

You have not had the easiest life but just remember, it is not how you start but where you finish. You have great potential, and I will be there with you, to guide you, and counsel you every step of the way to help you achieve all your dreams and goals. I love you.

And finally, to my beautiful wife, my best friend, my forever girl. You are the air for which I breathe. The first time we met at a Starbucks all those years ago, I knew at that moment you were the one, even after you walked out on me, lol.

Then I gave you an odd and peculiar proposal that thankfully you accepted. After that first night together, we have been inseparable ever since. They say relationships take work, but the truth is not when they are 100 percent just right.

This life, and what I do, would not be possible to get through without you by my side every step of the way. You are my best friend in this entire world and give me the inner strength I need to continue to try to make the world a better place for us all.

Thank you for your love, your loyalty, and your devotion. You are the last person I see when I go to bed at night and the first person I see when I wake up, and that is truly a blessing. Every day I get to spend with you by my side is better than the last. I love you.

About the Author

Josh Bernstein is an American talk show host, political analyst, commentator, author, and professional speaker. Josh is one of America's most sought-after television and radio guests. He has been called a "political savant" by the late legendary Hall of Fame broadcaster Barry Farber due to his almost encyclopedic breakdown on many of the important issues of our times.

Josh was the former national spokesman for the Association of Mature American Citizens (AMAC.US), which is one of America's leading seniors' health advocacy groups—with over two million members. As a highly in-demand guest, Josh delivers a unique and original perspective that is thought provoking, engaging, truthful, and well sourced.

His main areas of expertise include but are not limited to: world affairs, globalism, nationalism, health care, current events, social media, political trends, media bias, academia, immigration, and national security.

To find out more about Josh, please consider subscribing to his website at **www.jbushow.com** or **www.joshbernsteinuncensored.com** where Josh covers the news seven days a week with intellect and facts.